Yoga Therapy For Selected Diseases

Dr. M. M. GORE
Dr. D. R. VAZE
Dr. S. A. KULKARNI
Dr. J. P. OAK

KAIVALYADHAMA
Swami Kuvalayananda Marg,
Lonavla, Dist. Pune - 410 403,
Maharashtra, INDIA

Published on : 15 August 2008
Reprints on : May 2012
Reprints on : April 2017
Reprints on : March 2021

ISBN - 81-89485-49-0

Published by :
O.P. Tiwari, Secretary,
Kaivalyadhama, Swami Kuvalayananda Marg,
Lonavla, Dist. Pune - 410 403, Maharashtra, INDIA

Printed by :
UNIQUE OFFSET
50/7/A Dhayari Narhe Road,
Narhe Gaon,
Pune - 411 041

Price : ₹ 100/-

PREFACE

Today yoga has become more popular because of its potential to rejuvenate body-mind complex and to re-establish the healthy condition of the practitioner. Through scientific research it has been found that yoga is helpful in controlling stress disorders particularly essential hypertension, insomnia, hyperacidity, diabetes, asthma etc. However, the applied aspect of Asanas, Pranayama, Kriyas is not so easy to work out. It requires a qualified yoga therapist who would guide the patient once he knows the principles of yoga therapy.

The Ministry of health published a marvelous book 'Yoga therapy', written by Swami Kuvalayanand and Dr. S.L.Vinekar in 1963, Detailed information regarding the principles of yoga therapy and yoga techniques was given. The book is mainly useful for doctors who are interested in practicing yoga therapy. However, today people want to know in brief but easily and instantly about the diseases, symptoms and the yogic remedy. As warned by Hathayoga, if yogic practices are performed erroneously it would be quite dangerous to the individual. Knowing this and the need of today the present booklet has been brought out as a complementary publication.

Mostly the yoga therapy is misunderstood as a method consisting of few asanas and pranayama only, to cure any disease. Unfortunately this is not correct. On the contrary the yoga therapy is successful only when the patient understands and observes some of the important principles behind the concept of yoga therapy. The lifestyle changes are mandatory in combination with the prescribed yoga practice.

The idea of explaining these principles of yoga therapy in a lucid language and to provide at hand information about a few most common psychosomatic disorders along with the remedial part of yoga would be appreciated by the readers. The present booklet is a result of studious presentation from four authors who are related to yoga therapy and experts in their fields such as yoga research and naturopathy, modern medicine, Ayurveda, and psychology. We hope that readers will welcome this booklet and would reap the benefits. I congratulate all the four authors for their endeavor to write such a 'ready reference at hand' for patients, yoga therapists and teachers.

7th May 2008
Akshay Trittiya

Swamy Maheshananda
Chairman / Director,
K.S.M.Y.M. Samiti,
Swami Kuvalayananda Marg,
Kaivalyadhama, Lonavla - 410 403.

PART ONE

BASIC PRINCIPLES AND UNDERSTANDING OF YOGIC THERAPY

CONTENTS

INTRODUCTION

Where there is a health, there is happiness. Here the meaning of happiness is not the pleasure out of fulfillment of the desire but the jubilant feeling all the time that is free from fears and tensions. The primary objective of yoga is spiritual advancement and not to cure the diseases. However, it has been observed that many psychosomatic disorders are controlled best with the help of yoga practices and the persons who practice yoga regularly (*Sadhana*), can very well maintain their health, throughout their life. This indicates that the resistance power against the diseases i.e. immunity is improved due to the regular practice of yoga. The long life span of the yoga practitioners also indicates that the yoga practice can slow down the aging process. Today, many people are taking best advantage of this preventive and promoting aspect of yoga. There however is a growing tendency to apply yogic methods as the last resort for each and every disease, irrespective of its severity, duration and the age of the patient. This is however a wrong concept of yoga therapy.

Man has conquered the diseases like Malaria, Typhoid, Small pox and Tuberculosis arising out of infections caused by germs, bacteria, viri etc. But doctors and scientists have realized that in spite of good number of medicines, most sophisticated diagnostic tools and other medical facilities, it is difficult to cure the patients suffering from stress related disorders such as, Hypertension, Hyper-acidity, Insomnia, Heart diseases, Diabetes, Asthma, Arthritis, Spondylitis etc. with the conventional line of treatment. These disorders are even worse than usual infectious disorders. The human being has been challenged by these germless disorders. The reason is we often ignore the causative factors of these diseases.

Concept of health

As per WHO health does not mean merely an absence of disease but a jubilant feeling of well being at physical, mental, social and spiritual levels According to Ayurveda too the same message is seen:

समदोष समाग्निश्च समधातुः मलःक्रियाः ।
प्रसन्नात्मेंद्रियमनः स्वस्थ इत्यभिधीयते ।।

In short, when all the anatomical-physiological factors are in balanced condition and the mind, soul as well as sense organs are working in harmony, it is considered as a healthy state. Dissatisfaction or unhappiness in mind would cause imbalance in these factors. We know that in spite of all the luxuries at home, if the mind is dissatisfied we cannot enjoy anything. Happiness comes from within and does not depend on material gain or physical enjoyment (Nagarathna 1990). That is why the mental health is very important component of total health. Disturbances at the mental level can even alter the neuro-musculo-glandular mechanism of the body. It can also disturb the autonomic balance and hence the vital regulatory systems like cardio-vascular system, as well as endocrine system. The word 'to heal' is incorporated in the word 'health'. It indicates that the perfect healing is 'health'.

According to yoga health is an integrated state of body, mind and spirit. There is a harmony in all the psycho-physiological functions. It is well coordinated and balanced condition of body and mind wherein the homeostasis is adequately maintained. Therefore a feeling of happiness and contentment are essential factors of the sound health.

Concept of disease

When there is no balance between desire, need and the availability of money one feels dissatisfied. Out of dissatisfaction, frustration and dejection, stress is produced when there is a negative interaction between the self-projection and the surrounding environment. The self projection is influenced by our cravings, desires, likes and dislikes, attitudes, ambitions, beliefs, negative emotions, hopes and failures. Even our life-style is affected due to these factors.

The main reason is 'ignorance' on our part. Sloth (*styan*) and laziness (*alasya*) are other two *vikshepas*. The modern lifestyle, based on 'button technology' (remote control technology) makes us lazier. The way we eat, perform the exercises, take rest, play, behave with others, think, plan, sleep are all included under 'Life-style'. Most of the time, in a quest for maximum earning with minimum work, we choose wrong life-style. Sedentary working pattern, improper diet and irregular timings of food, inadequate rest and sleep and lack of exercise constitute wrong life-style. This will be further affected adversely by addictions to harmful habits like tobacco chewing, smoking and drinking alcohol. In addition, the environmental conditions, social, political and economical situations are constantly working on us, which again affect our mental state and physical health. With the imbalanced mind our responses to the incoming stimuli also go towards the negative direction. Sudden mental irritation or depression, frequently changing moods, lethargy, and mental dissatisfaction are the first signs of disturbed mind. Under such conditions our digestive system is greatly affected. General tone of the digestive musculature is disturbed.

It is known that the continuous stressful situation leads to sympathetic over-activity suggested by the raised levels of adrenaline and nor adrenaline. This causes spasm of the coronary arteries and an increase in cortisol level causing formation of blockages in the arteries speedily. Thus the stress, which is actually the normal defensive mechanism of the body to protect us in danger situations, now becomes harmful. The emotions play a significant role in our life. Positive emotions are constructive while negative emotions and emotional conflicts are destructive in nature. They produce disturbed condition of mind (*daurmanasya*) and also disturb the tone of the muscles including those of the blood vessels. This further impairs the vital autonomic functions like respiration, circulation, and glandular secretion and finally weakens the very immune process. Thus, the psychosomatic conditions slowly move from functional impairment to cellular disturbance and finally lead to the structural alteration (pathological changes). If this situation is not tackled early it leads to permanent organic changes in the various organs.

The effect of interpersonal stress on 20 women with rheumatoid arthritis (RA) was studied by Zautra (1999) and his colleagues. They found that there is an aggravation in RA following an increase in inter-personal stress. Women having stronger and positive marital relationship with their husbands were less affected. It is obvious from this study that the diseased condition is reversible if the stress is tackled correctly.

As it is observed in cases of diabetes mellitus, bronchial asthma, essential hypertension and rheumatoid arthritis that the conventional medical treatment can alleviate the symptoms and the patient also experiences the relief temporarily but the root cause of the disease remains mostly ignored.

Principles of Yoga therapy

In order to achieve and maintain the healthy condition, yoga lays emphasis on the following steps.

1. Purification of 'nadis' by removing the obstructing toxins from the body.
2. Reconditioning of the neuro-muscular and glandular system so that adequate immunity is regained.
3. Cultivation of proper psychological attitude so as to increase the ability of the individual to cope with the stressful situation if any.

It is wiser to wear a good quality shoes instead of removing nails and thorns spread on the road. Yoga is doing the same thing. Every living being is well equipped with the healing power. It is with us right from the birth. Yoga recuperates this natural strength of the body and mind to eliminate disturbing factors on the gross and subtler levels. Thus yoga supports and enhances this healing power by maintaining the equilibrium or homeostasis, through the development of optimum muscle tone, giving complete mental relaxation and constructing the proper emotional make-up. Along with the yogic therapy the main medicines from Ayurveda, Homeopathic or Allopathic systems may be continued, modified or stopped only on the advice of the respective treating physician.

Any variation in the results of the given yoga therapy will depend on the following two things.

1. Techniques of the yogic practices

For the desired effects from the yoga therapy one should ensure that the technique adopted is correct from the traditional as well as the scientific point of view. Our body responds as per the stimulus. Long lasting beneficial physiological changes will take place only when the proper techniques are repeated in the same sequence and at the same timing every day. The correctness of the technique may be checked with the experienced yoga therapist. Appropriate modification in the technique may be done by him/her for the particular patient as per his/her age and other conditions.

2. Constitution and nature of the patient

The disordered physical-mental-spiritual condition of the patient is known as *Prakriti.* The response of his body would depend on it. A yoga therapist should consider all the physical abilities and the psychological make-up, as well as, the limitations of the patients while deciding the line of yogic treatment. Most of the time, the preliminary reconditioning of the individual patient is necessary before starting the main yogic treatment.

Survey of the therapeutic research

Swami Kuvalayananda was the pioneer to investigate the effects of yogic practices on the scientific basis. These were the fundamental experiments in the field of yoga. Later on many scientists conducted the scientific researches in yoga. The applied research in the field of therapy was mostly carried out in the last 4 to 5 decades. Bhole, (1967 and 1979) revealed that **Asthma** could be controlled successfully in 69% patients with the yogic treatment in which vastra dhauti was found very effective. Datey, (1969) for the first time found the relaxative posture - shavasana as most effective for the management of **hypertension**. Later on Deshmukh, Dalvi, Vinekar, (1969), Patel, (1973) and Udupa (1980), not only confirmed these results but also further reported a reduction in catacholamine level after yogic therapy. Rajalaxmi also could treat 20 patients of hypertension effectively with Yoga. Gopal, (1973) has reported a significant improvement in blood pressure and respiratory functions after practicing yoga. Rajalaxmi treated 15 patients of bronchial Asthma with yogic treatment for 20 to 90 days and found that their vital capacity, PEFR and breath holding time was increased. On the basis of these investigations it seems that yoga helps asthmatics by improving their broncho-pulmonary functions and different respiratory capacities. It is also noticed that yoga therapy helps in removing the mental and emotional instability and establishes the balance in hormonal secretions. Parkodi, (1979) found that Shavasana practiced for 5 months could reduce blood pressure and catacholamine metabolism and improved adreno-cortical function. Tulpule, (1980) showed that a set of relaxative hathayogic postures could prevent myocardial infarction. Gore (1980) found that the air trapping observed in the spirogram of asthma patients was effectively removed immediately after practicing Vastra dhauti. Sharma, (1981) treated 27 patients of hypertension with shavasana for 2.5 months successfully PEFR of normal subjects was found to improve significantly after 45 days yogic training (Gore, 1981). Gore (1982) found that one-month yogic training could improve pulmonary functions of asthmatics.

Diabetes mellitus is another stress disorder where the number of patients is increasing day by day. After Udupa and Singh, (1972) reported significant reduction in blood sugar in normal subjects, many doctors came forward to conduct scientific studies on yogic treatment for diabetes. Koshti, (1972) studied serum proteins in diabetics before and after 6 weeks yogic treatment and found that A:G ratio was corrected along with the reduction in blood sugar. Melkote and Varandani, (1973) also reported promising results of yogic treatment for diabetes. Rugmini and Sinha, (1975) investigated 123 diabetics and found the yogic treatment effective in 64% patients. Gore, (1988) emphasized 15 min shavasana for two times along with other yoga postures for 45 days and found reduction in insulin intake from 44 units to 24 units.

Besides this, yoga therapy was also tried in other clinical conditions such as **Neuroticism** (Kocher, 1972), **Obesity** (Gharote, 1977), **Insomnia** (Joshi, 1979), **Mental retardation** (Rajalaxmi, 1979), **Epilepsy** (Parkodi, 1984), Udupa, Singh, 1984) and showed encouraging results. There was a comparative study on the effect of Yoga and Aerobics on **obesity** with 6 months follow up observations at Kaivalyadhama institute. The study revealed that yoga training was better in improving the level of health related fitness of obese patients in terms of reduced body weight and fat%, flexibility, hip girth and muscular strength (Bera, 2003). Both yoga as well as the aerobics training has beneficial effect towards reducing their blood pressure and heart rate in the age group of 35 to 60 years. The yogic treatment was more effective in case of residential group where diet regulation was also followed. Yoga was seen more effective in improving the respiratory efficiency than the aerobic exercise. The cardio-respiratory effect of yoga is long lasting and deeper as compared to aerobics (Gore 2004). Yoga regimen in residential group was found better than aerobic exercise in reducing anxiety in obese people (Bhogal and Oak 2005). Recently in Vivekananda Yoga Kendra, 18 patients of anxiety **neurosis** were treated with yoga therapy for 4 weeks. More emphasis was given on Pranayama and Shavasana. Increase in GSR, decrease in RR, increase in BHT and CE as well as, psychological status of the patients were observed. A sense of well-being and deeper relaxation was felt by all the patients. Udupa studied effect of yoga therapy for anxiety neurosis and has observed improvement after 3 months together with a reduction in the levels of acetylcholine and catacholamine in blood and urine. Wahia, after 6 weeks yogic treatment including meditation, has reported an improvement in 68% patients. Several studies have been reported on the yogic treatment for effective control of **spondylitis, backache, arthritis, rheumatism, menstrual disorders and gastro-intestinal disorders**. Since 1991, Yoga has been included in the rehabilitation program of the mentally challenged patients of the Govt. Mental hospitals at Thane and Nagpur.

For the individuals suffering from **Psychotic and neurotic depression** the results are encouraging such as reduction in restlessness, mental irritation and negative thinking. An improvement in mental concentration, sleep pattern and positive attitude was also observed after the practice of selected asanas, Anuloma viloma and Bhramari pranayama, Om recitation and Dhyana. Om recitation has been found to be the powerful psycho-physiological technique for calming and relaxing the mind (Bhogal, 1993 and Gore, 1997). Dean Ornish has proved that the **heart diseases** can be reversed and the bypass surgeries may be avoided when the patients follow the yogic life style. Improvement in cardiovascular efficiency due to one month yoga training was long back reported by Ganguly and Gharote, (1977). All these studies reveal that the yogic therapy has got a definite potential to heal the patients suffering from psychosomatic disorders due to its integrated approach.

Limitations of yogic therapy

Like any other therapy yoga therapy also has limitations. Truly speaking, we should consider it as a supporting therapy, which would help the healing process. Patience, experience, skill and zeal are very much required while treating various patients particularly the neurotics and the heart patients. Proper selection and application of yogic practices is very important. In case of patients of hysteria, psychosis and endogeneous depression, yoga therapist should not, normally, use yoga theraphy. In case of diseases like leprosy, cancer, malignant tumors, fibrosis, fractures, and severe structural or pathological changes, the yogic therapy is not advisable as a treatment but is definitely helpful to modify person's outlook towards the disease. However, yogic therapy is most effective in cases of psychosomatic diseases as mentioned earlier. It is an excellent preventive regime.

Supporting therapies

1. Observance of principles of *Astanga Yoga*

Patanjali Muni has recommended observance of *Yamas* and *Niyamas* of *Patanjali* for cultivation of correct mental attitude of the individual in relation to the self and with the society respectively and culturing the emotions. Eight fold approach of *Patanjali* brings about necessary changes in the mind body complex and its harmony.

Yamas include *Ahimsa* (non injury at the physical, mental and intellectual level), S*atya* (speaking and following the truth in all actions), *Asteya* (not taking the things which belong to others), *Brahmacharya* (not only celibacy or control in sex but also indicates interest in every aspect of education and to have balanced outlook regarding the success and failure in life) and *Aparigraha* (avoidance of unnecessary hoarding of objects).

Niyamas include *Shauch* (cleanliness at physical, mental and intellectual levels), *Santosh* (contentment in the present situation), *Tapa* (physical austerity and intellectual discrimination between what is good in the long run and the objects which give only temporary pleasure), *Swadhyay* (personal experience about the structure and functions of the body, as well as self study related to spiritual matters) and *Ishwar pranidhan* (offering all the credit to the almighty for one's achievements).

Our body has got energy in three forms. Jnana shakti (wisdom power), Kriya shakti (work power) and Ichchha shakti (will power). *Asanas* release and divert the energy from our upper and lower extremities to the internal organs in our abdomen, chest and brain. *Asanas* distribute this energy as per priority basis. This is achieved by raising the hands and legs from the ground or folding them together without a rise in pulse rate. The extra energy, produced by our internal organs is returned to our extremities during the relaxative asanas resulting in the increase of the endurance power of their muscles. *Asanas* are mainly centered upon the spinal column. This improves the conduction of neural impulses to the muscles, as well as, the blood supply to the spinal column. Increased blood supply provides adequate nutrients to all the muscles and joints and at the same time removes the toxins effectively. Alternate contractions and stretching of various muscles during cultural asanas give rise to alternate positive and negative pressure changes that stimulates various endocrine glands. A normal belief that a particular cultural *asana* is useful for a particular psychosomatic disorder is based on the wrong assumption that only a specific part of the body is affected by a specific *asana*. This however is not true as the benefits of *asanas* are collectively received by all the parts of the body.

Pranayama controls the energy supply to all the parts of the body with the help of voluntary regulation of the breathing. It balances and produces psychophysiological relaxtion by minimizing the tensions, leading to a stress free condition. Regular practice of *pranayama* not only improves breathing efficiency or capacity, co-ordination between CNS and ANS, concentration, will power and self-confidence but also strengthens the immune system. Pranayama reduces instability of mind, increases tolerance and patience in the practitioner that helps the healing power. Practice of *pranayama* leads one to *Pratyahara*. Here one learns the non-attachment with the usual sensory inputs which otherwise are quite troublesome.

Meditation increases the inner awareness. It develops a proper witnessing attitude by which one learns to accept the reality. It reduces the stress by tranquilizing the mind. It improves the mind – body coordination. The regular practitioner experiences the calmness, freshness and a feeling of well being throughout the day. This keeps one away from all the negative thinking and dwelling into the past incidences. *Meditation* increases the will power and rational thinking.

2. Approaches through Ayurveda

Ayurveda means the science of life. It has two fold objectives.

स्वस्थस्य स्वास्थ्य रक्षणम् ।

"Swasthasya swasthya-rakshanam"

It means preservation and promotion of health in healthy individual.

And the other objective is,

विकार परिमोक्षः ।

vikar parimokshah

It means to cure the diseases and to recover the patient to normal health.

Ayurveda is based on some basic principles, out of which one important principle is,

Tridosha siddhanta

Tridosha viz. *vata, pitta and kapha* are the humors which constitute the structure of the body and regulate all the functions.

Ayurveda emphasizes that the balance of these three principles maintains the health. 'Prakruti' i.e. 'Human Constitution' is well explained in Ayurveda. *Tridoshas* influence all the physiological and psychological activities of the body. Thus 'Prakruti' plays very important role in health, disease, emotions and all aspects of life. This makes essential for every individual to know his or her constitution. On the basis of this knowledge of *Prakriti*, an Ayurvedic physician can advise the specific diet, which is helpful to preserve the health and prevent the diseases.

As emphasized in Ayurvedic texts for preservation of health, special *Dina-charya* and *Ritu-Charya*. i.e.

Daily and Seasonal Regimens are described as the important guidelines for us.

Daily routine (*Dina charya*)

First of all make it a habit to wake up early in the morning before sunrise and attend nature's call followed by abhyanga snana and the moderate exercise. Before lunch see that not only children, elders or the servants have taken the food but even the pet animals like cows; dogs etc have received their food.

Seasonal adaptations (*Ritu charya*)

There are three seasons of the year, subdivided in six ritus of two months each. The life style should be modified according to these ritus. e.g. in *Hemanta* ritu i.e November and December, the appetite is generally strong to digest nourishing food such as sweets, fruits, ghee, milk, butter. One should therefore take best advantage of this opportunity according to the strength of the digestive fire. Oil massage, hot water bath, moderate exercise and sex enjoyment are recommended for this season. On the contrary in *Grishma* ritu i.e. in April and May it is just opposite.

Massage

Now a days, we are familiar with various types of massage treatments. If we want to get its best benefits then it is important to know the scientific as well as traditional concepts of massage. Massage is known as "Snehan" in Ayurveda. Massage is not only the application of oil but it has a special technique with medicinal oils. It is of various types.

Basic types of massage (*Snehan*) are,

1. Abhyanga

Abhyanga means application of Medicinal Oil all over the body. This treatment is of great value in maintenance & improvement of one's beauty in terms of important features like good complexion, overall healthy & attractive personality. *Abhyanga* helps to achieve good complexion by improving the blood circulation and also brings about effective Vata-prashamana (as skin is one of the seats of vata dosha). *Abhyanga snana* means a light oil massage followed by bath. It increases freshness and one feels calm and pleasant for the whole day. If a massage is done in the evening, it improves quality of sleep.

Vitiated *vata* creates roughness, dryness and darkness of the skin. Not only this, but *vata* is a unique stimulant factor for all the functions of the body and mind. The massage treatment, gives feeling of activeness, freshness and also brings about the relaxation of mind. It gives proper relief from physical exertion. Therefore it is advocated as a daily regimen.

2. Udvartana

Udvartana means rubbing medicinal powders over body. It is the best treatment to cleanse the skin and also to reduce the extra fat.

3. Shirobhyanga

It means application of oil on head. As the head is the important seat of 'Jñāendriyas' (sense organs), application of medicinal oil improves the strength of sense organs. It also improves memory and intelligence and relieves mental stress. It is the best treatment in sleep disorders. If done regularly, it strengthens hair and also improves its quality.

4. Shiro-pichu Dharana

It means keeping a piece of cotton soaked in oil on the

head. If one is not able to do head massage, then he or she can avail this treatment.

5. Padabhyanga

It is the oil massage given to the soles. It removes dryness, numbness and pain in legs. It strengthens the calf muscles. Regular Padabhyanga gives soothing effect to eyes and helps to improve the vision.

Regarding the curative aspect of Ayurveda, the treatments are classified into two types.

1. ***Shamana*** i.e. balancing the disturbed *tridosha* with the help of medicines and diet.
2. ***Shodhana*** i.e. to remove vitiated *tridosha* from the body that are main causes of disease. This is known as *Panchakarma* treatment.

A therapeutic procedure practiced as a major speciality is called '*Rasayana*' i.e. Rejuvenation or Vitalization. It is the best way to prevent aging and impart longevity. These treatments are also useful to enhance immunity against disease and to improve the physical, as well as the mental health of an individual.

3. Approach through Naturopathy

Sun Therapy

Sun bath (***Surya snana)*** in early morning just after the sun rise for 5-7 minutes is very beneficial. Vitamin D is produced underneath the skin with the help of ultraviolet rays present at the time of sunrise. It improves the resistance power of the body and also influences the health of our eyes, skin and helps the growth of the bones favorably.

Mud therapy

The earth (***Mrittika***) is cleaned and a paste is prepared by adding water. This paste of mud is applied on the skin, abdomen or any painful part. When the paste dries, it is removed and cold water bath is taken. It is useful in case of skin diseases, constipation, and increased heat of the body.

Water therapy

Water is used amply in Naturopathy and Ayurveda (***Jala chikitsa***). Enema, Tub bath, Hipbath, steam bath, Magnetic water therapy needs large quantity of water. Napkin, soaked in hot and cold water, is used alternately for reducing inflammation and pain of the joints.

4. Other Supporting measures

Changing the lifestyle

Generally it is found that the patient undergoes yoga practices for an hour in the morning and spends rest of the day as he was spending previously in his own way. Modifying and changing the lifestyle is an integral and most vital part of the yogic therapy. He must consult his yoga therapist, doctor and make suitable changes in his lifestyle. This is required for constructing the correct psychological attitude so that the stress factors are best tackled and nullified.

Bhagwad Gita says,

युक्ताहार विहारस्य युक्तचेष्टस्य कर्मसु
युक्त स्वप्नावबोधस्य योगोभवति दुःखहा ।

Yuktahar viharasya yuktachestasya karmasu,
Yukta swapnavabodhasya yogobhavati duhkhaha

That is, just enough diet, work, sleep, wakeful state, entertainment or sport will remove the grievances and one will become happy. This principle of a moderation in every aspect of life is very important which is mostly overlooked by us.

Diet

Sattvik diet means pure, light, fresh and yet nutritive diet that is necessary after fasting. White pumpkin, cauli flower, palak, mung dal, fresh coconut, cucumber, coriander, jeera are some of the items of the Sattvik diet. The food is mostly simple and boiled one. Pickles, papad or spices are not allowed. Such diet is taken for 3-4 days after the fasting. In yoga, even the garlic and onion are not allowed.

Mitahara

Taking food in less quantity, even less than the appetite is always beneficial. This concept is found in Ayurveda and also in Yoga. It is suggested that one should fill his stomach just half and leave the space for water and the air. By doing this it is thought that the digestion would be completed nicely and would improve the digestive power (***Agni***). This will provide good nutrition to the body and the bile secretion will be balanced.

Ayurveda also believes that body -mind - soul complex forms the basic tripod of health and suggests ***Sadachar*** (good or ideal behaviour). It is known as the proper life-style in modern age.

Mild exercise

Movement is the life. Without movement there is no life. Brisk walking, jogging, yoga, swimming, morning walk, mild callisthenic exercises are important to keep one fit physically and mentally. Regular light exercise for 30 to 45 min, preferably in the morning will,

1. Make you feel more energetic, enthusiastic through out a day. It enables better use of oxygen in the body.
2. Increases resistance to various infectious diseases. Delays onset of fatigue and increases cardio-vascular endurance.
3. Tones up the muscles, glands, and venous return. Increases stamina and relieves muscular tension. Trains and prepares the muscles for day-to-day life activities.
4. Improves efficiency of heart, lungs and other organs like joints of the body by increasing blood circulation to them. Removes waste products efficiently from these organs.
5. Reduces cholesterol and maintains blood pressure at normal level.
6. Appetite, digestion, evacuation (bowel movement) are properly adjusted with the other body activities and needs.

7. Improves sleep pattern. Ensues sound sleep.
8. Helps in coping with stress, tension, anxiety or depression and keeps you in pleasant and fresh mood all the time. Naturally then you remain away from worries.
9. Increases memory and concentration as well as the creativity.
10. Increase a feeling of well-being.

From this it is obvious that the exercise should not be of exhaustive but refreshing in nature. Hatha-yogic practices like *asanas, kriyas* seem to be fit for this purpose as is evident from the research findings. They also have curative effect. They maintain the energy level throughout a day.

Proper behaviour or mental culture (*Sad-vritta*)

Ayurveda insists upon cultivation of an ideal attitude so that one leads a *satvik* type of life i.e. selfless, simple and pure life. Charaka says 'be noble and honest in your thoughts and deeds. Have compassion for the weak and poor. Have patience and forgiveness. Speak moderately and softly. Avoid self torture and self praising. Maintain equanimity in the success and failure, pleasure and pain etc.

Prevent negative feelings and emotions like hate, envy, anger, jealous and cultivate the positive emotions like love, faith, devotion and friendship for all. This will keep you away from the psychic and nervous disorders.'

Proper Sleep, rest and relaxation

Sleep is the most basic and natural need of every living creature. The central nervous system requires a proper rest after continuous conscious physical or mental work. Children need 10 to 12 hours sleep while an adult would need only 6 to 8 hours sleep in 24 hours. Sound sleep makes us refreshed and energetic for further work. Most of the healing processes are taking place during the sound sleep. Injuries like fracture, skin ruptures, muscle tear, and scratches are healed during sleep. Rest and sleep are important components of the rehabilitation programme.

Rational thinking and entertainment

Any kind of agitation or irritation in mind or nervousness is an obstacle for the healing process and hence the illness will be prolonged. Illness is a state of disequilibrium while peace is a prerequisite for establishing equilibrium. Peace is a powerful static and defensive inner force assisting the healing process. Whenever a doctor advises a complete physical rest it really means the mental peace. If mind is peaceful the breathing rate and the heart rate are slow. Positive thinking and mental peace are essentials for the spiritual development also. Quietude is a positive strength. Rejuvenation, reorganization, putting everything into order is only possible when there is a peace. Calmness indicates an absence of instability or conflicts in mind. Autonomic balance is established when there is peace in mind. Therefore the patient should remain aware that an inner peace is experienced for maximum duration all through out a day. Strong emotions, negative thinking, hatred, disappoint-ment, dissatisfaction, muscular strain or fatigue can stir the mental peace and diminish immunity. On the contrary appropriate recreation through entertainment, humor, laughter is indispensable for joyfulness and happiness. They perform their role as analgesics and accelerate the recovery.

Deep faith and devotion

These are also positive inner forces assisting in developing and maintaining the proper mental attitude and psychological composure. This builds up strong foundation for the yoga therapy. Deep faith (*Shraddha*) and devotion (*Bhakti*) are also essential to enhance the inner peace and patience, which would support the healing process. Believe in our *Rishi-Munis* who have developed wonderful yoga system for us and always remain thankful to them.

REFERENCES

1. **Bera, T.K., Gore, M.M.** and **Oak, J.P.** (1998), 'Recovery from stress in two different postures and in shavasana', Ind.J.of physiol.Pharmaol Vol 42:2, 473-478
2. **2. Bera, T.K., Gore, M.M., Kulkarni, D.D., Bhogal, R.S. and Oak, J.P.(2003)**, 'Residential and Non-residential yoga training on health related physical fitness of obese patients', *Yoga Mimamsa,* Vol 34: 3&4, 166-187.
3. **Bhogal, R.S., Gore, M.M.** and **Rajapurkar, M.V.** (1993), 'Effect of low pitched Om recitation on some selected psychological parameters' Yoga Mimamsa, Vol 31:4, 159-175

4. **Bhogal, R.S., Oak, J.P., Gore, M.M., Kulkarni, D.D., and Bera, T.K.(2005)**,' Effect of a month long training programme of yoga and aerobics on anxiety in obese Indians', *Yoga Mimamsa,* Vol 36: 3, 153-162.
5. **Bhole, M.V and Karambelkar, P.V.** and **Gharote M.L.** (1970), 'Effect of yoga practices on vital capacity', Ind.J.Chest Dis. 12:1&2, 32-35
6. **Datey, K.K., Deshmukh, S.N.** and **Dalvi, C.P.** (1969) 'Shavasana -a yogic exercise in the management of hypertension', Angiology, 20, 325-333
7. **Dean Ornish,** 'Program for Reversing heart disease', IVY Books, USA (1996)
8. **Desiraju, T.** (1989), 'Effect of meditations and pranayamas in promoting homeostasis in normal individuals', Yoga Mimamsa, Vol 28:2, 1-3
9. **Ganguly, S.K.** and **Gharote, M.L.** (1974), 'Cardiovascular efficiency before and after yogic training', Yoga Mimamsa, Vol 17:1, 89-97
10. **Gharote, M.L.** (1977), 'An evaluation of the effects of yogic treatment on obesity', Yoga Mimamsa Vol 14:1, 13-37
11. **Gopal, K.S.** et al (1973), 'Effect of yogasanas and pranayamas on blood pressure, pulse rate and some respiratory functions', Ind.J.Physiol and Pharmaco, 17:3, 273-276
12. **Gore, M.M.** (1981), 'Effect of yogic training on peak flow rate', Yoga Mimamsa,Vol 20:1 and 2, 100-104.
13. **Gore, M.M.** (1982), 'Effect of Yogic treatment on some pulmonary functions in Asthmatics', Yoga Mimamsa, Vol 20:4, 51-58

14. **Gore, M.M.** and **Bhole, M.V.** (1983), 'Respiratory responses to Vastra dhauti in Asthmatics', Yoga Mimamsa, Vol 22:1&2, 47-53

15. **Gore, M.M.** (1987), 'Yogic treatment for diabetes' Yoga Mimamsa Vol 26:3&4, 130-146

16. **Gore, M.M.** (1988), 'Effect of yogic training on neuro-muscular efficiency in normal and stressful conditions', Yoga Mimamsa, Vol 26: 2&3, 15-24

17. **Gore, M.M.** (1990), 'Effect of Trataka on various psycho-physiological functions', Yoga Mimamsa, Vol 29:3, 1-15

18. **Gore, M.M.** (1997), 'Physiological responses to two different types of Aum recitation', Yoga Mimamsa, Vol 32:1&2, 1-7

19. **Gore, M.M**. (2003), 'Effect of yoga and aerobics training on cardio-respiratory functions in obese people', *Yoga Mimamsa*, Vol 35:1&2, 35-53.

20. **Kaplan, J.R.** et. al (1982), 'Social status, environment and atherosclerosis in cynomolgus monkeys', Arteriosclerosis, 2:5, 359-68

21. **Kocher, H.C.** (1972), 'A study of yogic practices as a variable in Neuroticism, anxiety and hostility', Yoga Mimamsa, Vol 15:2, 37-46

22. **Koshti** et al (1972), 'Electrophoretic pattern of serum proteins in diabetes mellitus as influenced by physical exercises-yogasanas', J.Mysore Med. Asso 36, pp64

23. **Nagarathna, R., Nagendra, H.R.** and **Robin Monro,** 'Yoga for common ailments' Gaia Books limited, London, 1990

24. **Oak, J.P.** and **Bhole, M.V.** (1988), 'Therapy based on yogic principles and techniques: neurotic depression and inguinal hernia', Yoga Mimamsa, Vol 27:1&2, 75-85

25. **Oak, J.P., Bhogal,R.S., Gore, M.M., Kulkarni, D.D., and Bera, T.K.(2004)**, 'Effect of month long programme of yoga ad aerobics on some factors of anxiety in obese Indians: a qualitative study', *Yoga Mimamsa*, Vol 36:3, 153-162.

26. **Patel, C.H.** (1973), 'Yoga and biofeedback in the management of hypertension', The Lancet, Nov. 10, 1053-1055

27. **Patel, C.H., Marmot, M.G.** and **Carruthers, M.** (1985), 'Trial of relaxation in reducing coronary risk: four year follow up', British Med.J. 290,1103-6

28. **Pedro de vicente** (1987), 'Role of yoga therapy in anxiety, neurosis and depression', Yoga Mimamsa, Vol 26:3&4, 1-14

29. **Roldan, E.** and **Dostalek C.** (1985), 'EEG patterns suggestive of shifted levels of excitation, effected by hathayogic exercises', Activ. Nerv. Sup. (Praha), 27:2, 81-88

30. **Rugmini, P.S.** and **Sinha, R.N.** (1976), 'Effect of yoga therapy in Diabetes mellitus', Seminar on Yoga, science and man, CCRIMH, p175-189

31. **Swami Kuvalayananda** and **Vinekar, S.L.** 'Yoga therapy',

32. **Tulpule, T.H.** (1977), 'Yogic exercises and diabetes mellitus', J. Diab. Asso.India Vol 17.

33. **Udupa, K.N.**, 'Stress and its management by Yoga', Varanasi press, (1980), 305-320

34. **Zautra, A.J.** et al (1998), 'An examination of individual difference in the relationship between interpersonal stress and disease activity among women with rheumatoid arthritis', Arthritis Care Res. Aug 11:4, 271-279.

PART TWO

YOGIC THERAPY FOR SELECTED DISEASES

1. ARTHRITIS

Arthritis is most common of all disabling diseases affecting one out of 10 people. It is a crippling degenerative process that leads to irreversible destructive disorder. There is an inflammation of joints, pain, stiffness, redness, heat and loss of function in one / or more joints. Most affected joints are, the weight bearing joints of spine, hips, knees, ankles and fingers. Most common forms are,

1. Osteo-arthritis
2. Gouty Arthritis
3. Rheumatoid Arthritis
4. Acute Rheumatic Arthritis.

1. Osteo-arthritis

This is due to chronic degenerative condition of bones, commonly seen in middle and old age. It is related with the degeneration of articular cartilage of the weight bearing joints or formation of osteophytes.

Causes

Overweight due to wrong diet, lack of exercise, calcium deficiency, imbalance in the parathyroid function, mental and emotional stress, and sedentary life style and wear and tear of the joint tissue from early injury to joint or osteophytes formation are the major causes.

Symptoms

There is a stiffness, pain and loss of flexibility of the joint.

2. Gouty Arthritis

This chronic or acute form of arthritis is associated with gout due to metabolic disorder.

Joint of big toe is the most susceptible part. In chronic cases it damages the kidneys.

Causes

Excessive uric acid accumulated in the blood and deposits of urates of sodium around the joints. Excessive consumption of red meat and coffee.

Signs and Symptoms

Fever, headache, tenderness, swelling and formation of nodes on the joints. Patient will complain restricted and painful movements. Skin becomes tense, reddish and warm. Pain increases at night.

3. Rheumatoid Arthritis

This is severe, crippling and rapidly progressive form of joint degeneration often found in young and middle aged people. It is found more in women than men. Inflammatory changes bring about the structural deformities as a result of autoimmune reaction.

Causes

Specific cause is not known. Severe emotional shock and stress may trigger it. Acute infection. Above-mentioned changes in joints are due to an antigen - antibody reaction of own body tissue.

Sign and Symptoms

Swelling and pain give rise to restriction of joint movement. Pain becomes localized with fever and malaise, 'morning stiffness', pain and tenderness and swelling of the entire joint. If not properly attended, it leads to destruction of joint tissue and deformities of joints. Psychological disturbances are found to aggravate the disorder.

Typical personality changes

These chronic arthritic changes give rise to depression and the patient becomes nervous, tense, worried, and moody. Suppression of anger and other emotions aggravate symptoms further.

4. Acute Rheumatic Arthritis

Usually it occurs in low-income group due to unsuitable living environment such as damp and wet walls and floor of the house. Major joints of the body are affected.

Causes

Viral infections like cold and flu that is superimposed by streptococcal infection.

Signs and Symptoms

Stiffness and pain in the body parts especially in joints. Symptoms subside when the toxins are removed from the body or the infection is overcome. Duration of symptoms is generally short. This has a strong susceptibility of involving the heart valves. It is said about this condition 'it leaks the joint and bites the heart'.

Treatment

Yoga practices are to be practiced by the individual, only when the acute condition subsides. Sufficient bed rest, suitable medicines, corrections in food habits and lifestyle are essential for getting optimum results.

Following yoga practices are recommended.

Asanas

Asanas would require the modification to suit the flexibility and the overall physical condition of the patient. Depending on the joints involved the asanas should be selected from the following.

Pavanmuktasana, Ardha-halasana, Setubandh-asana, Marjar-asana, Akarna Dhanurasana, Chakrasana (Sideward bending), Utkatasana, Tadasana, Vakrasana

Shuddhikriyas

Laghu / Purna Shankha-prakshalana, Kunjal/Vaman, Neti, Kapalabhati.

Pranayama

Anuloma-viloma, Bhastrika, Shitali

Om Recitation

Diet

Take a simple and light diet. Avoid sour fruits, curd, pickles, spices, milk and dairy products. Eat fresh fruits and boiled, as well as, sprouted pulses like moong. Auto urine therapy is also recommended.

Points to be noted

(1) Consult your doctor if the vague, shifting pain persists for more than 8 days.

(2) If R.A. factor test of the blood is positive, control the diet and take regular exercises.

(3) Accept Yoga as a life style with regularity and patience and not as a temporary relief from the present symptoms.

(4) In acute phase, when severe pain is experienced, take necessary medicines and proper rest. After acute phase is over, start practicing asanas under the proper guidance.

(5) Do not suppress the pain with painkillers.

2. ASTHMA

Earlier it was said that Asthma is a disease, which can never be cured completely and that it leaves the patients only on their death. It is primarily a disease of the respiratory system. Here, the patient has more difficulty in expiration than inspiration. There is a wheezing, cough and a sense of suffocation. The attack of asthma may last for a few minutes to few hours or even days wherein the patient is exhausted. It is common to all ages, children and adolescents of both sexes, irrespective of socio-economic background.

Causes

Asthma may be hereditary. Patient is allergic to pollen grain, food products, dust, animal hair, drugs, air pollution, industrial smoke and diesel fumes, milk and dairy products. Suppression of negative emotions like jealousy, anger, resentment, hatred, are often precipitating causes. So also loneliness, emotional hypersensitivity, fear of rejection, super ego consciousness are the other precipitating factors. Due to short breath, CO_2 is not expelled completely from the body. Constipation and indigestion may be associated with accumulation of toxins leading to asthmatic attack.

Signs and Symptoms

Premonitory symptoms are usually sneezing, nasal irritation and nose block. Accumulation of mucus in the bronchi gives rise to obstruction in breathing that produces a feeling of burden over chest. Spasm may be present in chest leading to the difficulty in breathing. Patient gasps for breath and nails and lips become blue indicating less oxygen supply. Difficulty in breathing makes patient unable to lie down in the bed and compels the patient to sit in propped up position with support. Exhaustion in breathing leads to sweating. Distress and anxiety increases due to laborious breathing. Eosinophil count in blood increases. Mucus secretion becomes thick and sticky. The chest becomes hyper-expanded and the lungs hyper-inflated. So the person has to do expiration with efforts, which becomes very short. Inspiration is also shallow and short. Longer the struggle for breath more is the severity of the attack, distress and anxiety. The asthmatic is unable to relax. He is exhausted and develops the flexion attitude of the body in a defense.

Yogic Treatment

Main focus is on the restoration of depleted and blocked pranic energy channels through shuddhi kriyas, asanas, and pranayamas in attack free condition. Yogic treatment reduces the intensity of attack and increases the gap between two attacks. It enhances the stamina, endurance and reduces hyperacidity.

Kriyas : Neti, Dhauti (specially Vamana and Vastra dhauti), Kapalabhati,

Asanas

Sarvangasana or Viparitakarani, Ardha and purna halasana, Matsyasana, Pavanmuktasana, Bhujangasana, Makarasana, Ardha-shalabhasana, Vakrasana, Parvatasana, Ushtrasana, Gomukhasana, Chakrasana, Tadasana, Shavasana according to the flexibility of the spine and physical capacity of the individual. Practice of Surya-namaskar is also helpful.

Mudras : Brahmamudra, Simhamudra.

Bandhas : Uddiyana, Agnisara (Mild)

Pranayama : Anuloma-Viloma, Bhastrika, Bhramari, and Ujjayi.

Om recitation : (10 times or more)

Points to be noted:

(1) Do not neglect the attack. Take necessary medicine

(2) Do not perform any yoga practice during acute attack.

(3) Regularity, patience and perseverance and belief in yoga practices is necessary.

(4) Express your emotions, do not suppress them. Think positively.

(5) Have light and easily digestible diet. Avoid milk and milk products, rice, curd, banana, sour fruits and fried items.

(6) Prevent constipation.

(7) Learn to recognize initial symptoms of asthmatic attack and practice Jalaneti / Sutraneti,

Vamana dhauti and relaxation. This will subside the attack / reduce the intensity of attack.

(8) Remain engaged in some constructive work.

(9) Avoid cold drinks and sudden exposure to cold weather. Drink warm water instead of frequent tea or coffee.

3. HERNIA

Hernia is the protrusion of any internal organ through an abnormal or weak opening of the peritoneum covering. E.g. Due to weak abdominal wall the intestinal part protrudes. It is found in both sexes. Some of the important types of hernia are as follows.

1. Inguinal hernia

It is very common in men than women. About 70% of the hernia patients are suffering from inguinal hernia. It occurs when a part of abdominal viscera pushes into inguinal canal. Inguinal hernia usually results from non-closure of the peritoneal fold entering into scrotum.

2. Femoral hernia

It is found in 17 % of the patients of hernia. It usually occurs in women. The bowel part (intestine) enters in to the front side of the thigh through femoral ring.

3. Umbilical hernia

Occurrence is about 8% of total hernias. The hernial sac bulges out at the umbilicus (navel) where abdominal muscles are weak. This hernia occurs at birth, infancy, in obese and middle aged people having weak abdominal muscles.

1. **Reducible Hernia**
   Where the protruded sac can be pushed back inside the abdomen, it reduces itself when the person lies down, but re-emerges on standing.

2. **Irreducible Hernia**
   It is a dangerous, life-threatening situation and needs

surgical treatment. This occurs when protruded abdominal contents cannot be pushed back into its normal position. Obstructed loops of intestine may lead to gangrene and if the surgical intervention is not performed in time may lead to death of the individual.

Causes

Congenital absence of the anterior abdominal wall leads to protrusion of all abdominal contents, which is known as exomphalus major. This usually ends fatally. It may occur due to sudden jerky movements while lifting the heavy weight from the ground. Increased intra abdominal pressure resulting from long lasting cough, straining during defecation or passing urine also contributes to hernia specially when prostate enlargement is present. Constipation, flabbiness, lack of exercise and sedentary life style are also some of the causes.

Signs and Symptoms

Patient complains of pain and heaviness in abdominal area. Patient is unable to stand, sit, walk or sleep comfortably when the hernia gets obstructed and becomes restless when projectile vomiting starts.

Treatment

Commonly it is dealt with the surgery or mechanical support with belt. The management will depend on nature and severity of hernia. Asanas are of some help before the weakness of the abdominal wall becomes marked. Tackling of the conditions like constipation, obstruction in passing urine and chronic cough are essential before surgical treatment of hernia is carried out.

Asanas

Bhadrasana, Ardha-halasana, Viparitakarani, Pavanmuktasana, Yoga mudra, (in padmasana), Naukasana (in supine position), Setubandhasana, and Shavasana (for 20 minutes). Any asana leading to abdominal pressure on natural opening of the peritoneum should be avoided.

Other Practices

Uddiyana and Agnisara (mild and in supine position), Anuloma-viloma pranayama and Om recitation.

Points to be noted

1) Avoid constipation, indigestion, and gas formation.
2) Lift the weight in a proper way.
3) Perform regular exercises to strengthen the abdominal muscles.

4. Spondylosis and Spondylitis

Spondylosis

It is an ankylosing condition of the spine, which may occur even at an age of 20 years. Slow development of ankylosing condition does not produce severe symptoms however if it develops rapidly it causes narrowing of the disc space. The nerve passing through the intervertebral foramina is compressed, giving rise to pain and also causes various other complications like stiffness of the spinal joints.

Spondylitis

It is an inflammation of one or more vertebrae thereby reducing the joint space and compressing the peripheral nerve. The stiffness and the immobility of the spine also increase if the condition does not come under control and slowly degenerative changes continue to occur. These two disorders, commonly referred to as Spondylitis are not normally differentiated. The common age group suffering from this condition is middle age, having prolonged sitting jobs.

Three major types of Spondylitis are

1. CERVICAL
2. LUMBAR
3. ANKYLOSING SPONDYLITIS.

1. Cervical Spondylitis

It is characterized by pain and spasm of muscle in upper

back, back of the neck and back of the head. There is a stiffness of the neck region, restricting the movements of the neck and head. It causes gradual degenerative process or wear and tear of the joints, bones, muscles and ligaments of the neck.

Causes

Usual cause is osteo-arthritis of the vertebral bones in the neck region. It might have developed after whiplash injury in the past. Precipitating cause may be habit of using thick pillow during sleep. Similarly sitting on table job in an improper posture also may lead to cervical Spondylitis.

Signs and Symptoms

Tension headache, restriction of neck movements from stiffness and pain in the neck region. Muscular weakness is due to degenerative changes in the muscles. Giddiness and ringing in ear are due to affection of the vestibular apparatus in the ear. New dense bony projection (osteophytes) and narrowing of disk space can be seen in X rays. The atherosclerosis of the vertebral arteries decreases the blood flow to the brain. Bony overgrowth in the vertebrae may compress the cervical nerve roots, resulting in radiating pain in arms (upper arm, lower arm, fingers), numbness and heaviness.

2. Lumbar Spondylitis

Degenerative changes take place at lumbar region i.e. in lower back (mostly 4th or 5th vertebra) leading to nerve compression.

Causes

Degenerative changes gives rise to narrowing of the disc space that can also occur due to accidental injuries, compressing the nerve root. spasm of the muscles of the lower back region leads to bad posture, which in turn aggravates the spasm further.

Signs and Symptoms

There is a pain in the lumbar region. Restriction of forward bending of the back, heaviness, numbness, cramps in legs and tingling sensation results from compression of the spinal nerve. Inability to walk for long distance, inability to stand or sit for long time compels one to restrict all the activities.

3. Ankylosing Spondylitis

It usually leads to total stiffness of the back restricting all movements due to pain. This condition also occurs in the middle aged people.

Causes

Exact cause is not known but usually weak muscles of the back, constant wrong sitting posture, heredity, extra calcium intake, lack of exercise or movements are blamed to produce this disability.

Signs and Symptoms

Stiff back leads to inability to turn the neck and therefore patient has to turn whole body to look back. Pain persists in upper / lower and /or middle back. Patient is unable to sit, stand or even sleep comfortably for a long time due to pain and heaviness in legs.

Treatment

Asanas

Asanas are practiced to strengthen the back muscles and to improve their flexibility. Asanas provide natural traction. It helps to reduce the pain caused by compression of the nerve root. The selection from the following asanas is advised according to the site of the defect.

Pavanamuktasana, Ardha-halasana, Setubandh-asana, Naukasana (in prone pose), Makarasana, Niralambasana, Ardha-shalabhasana, Vakrasana, Brahma Mudra, Parvatasana, Bhadrasana, Yogamudra, Shashankasana, Chakrasana (Sideward bending), Supta-tadasana,

Kriyas : Agnisara (mild)

Pranayama : Anuloma-Viloma pranayama.

Om chanting.

Points to be noted:

(1) Learn the yogic practices from proper yoga therapist. Take complete rest if there is acute pain.

(2) Practice regularly Shavasana / Makarasana in between two asanas which is helpful to bring beneficial results.

(3) Practice 15 to 20 min. Shavasana at the end.

(4) Do not perform any movement hurriedly.

(5) Practice with patience and regularity.

Follow these instructions and avoid thick pillow during sleep in all the three types of Spondylitis.

5. SCIATICA AND SLIPPED DISC

Sciatica and Slipped Disc are two closely related painful conditions. Slipped disc occurs mostly in the lower back / lumbar region due to overstraining while lifting the weight from the ground, or traumatic injury to the back.

Sciatica

There is severe pain along the course of the sciatic nerve starting from the lower back and traveling down the leg up to toes.

Causes

The common causes present are injury or inflammation of the nerve or the nerve root resulting from metabolic, toxic or infectious disorders. Secondly it may occur because of the compression of nerve root due to ruptured intervertebral disc by the prolapse of the pulp of the disc. It may also occur due to sudden jerk in the lower back while lifting the weight or by sudden movement. Pregnant women may experience this problem resulting from awkward position maintained for long time. Patients of Diabetes Mellitus are prone to this condition as a result of neuritis if the blood sugar is not properly maintained.

Signs and Symptoms

1) There is a shooting pain in the lower back region and radiating to the inner side of the thigh, back of the knee, calf muscles, ankles and toes.
2) There is a heaviness / numbness in the leg.
3) Tingling or pinprick sensation in the legs is also felt by some patients.
4) Movement of legs is troublesome.

5) Symptoms are worse at night and in stormy weather.
6) Leg raising test of the affected side is positive on extending the foot.

Treatment

During acute condition patient needs rest in bed. Patients are advised to walk by taking short steps and putting the complete feet on the ground. Suitable asanas may be selected from the following list of asanas.

Asanas

1. Pavanmuktasana with one and two legs
2. Ardha-halasana
3. Makarasana
4. Ardha Shalabhasana
5. Brahmamudra
6. Parvatasana
7. Vakrasana
8. Bhadrasana
9. Janu Shirasana
10. Utkatasana
11. Tadasana
12. Chakrasana (Sideward bending in standing)
13. Shavasana

Shuddhikriya

Agnisara (mild) in supine position with folded legs is advised.

Pranayama

Anuloma Viloma Pranayama is found beneficial in sciatic patients.

Om recitation

SLIPPED DISC

Human Vertebrae are linked with each other with the discs, which act like shock absorbers of the spine. Generally, the slipped disc occurs in lower back at L_4 - L_5 or L_5 - S_1 level. There is a posterior displacement of part of an intervertebral disc, giving rise to the compression of the peripheral nerve.

Causes

Most common cause is sudden jerky movement of the lower back while lifting the heavy weight from the floor without bending over the knees. It may also happen due to sudden rise of pressure during sneezing or injury to the spine from the weeding or shoveling in the garden. It usually occurs in people having weak back muscles from sedentary life style.

Signs and Symptoms

Severity of symptoms depends upon extent of the disc prolapsed. This makes the person immobile and finds it difficult to become straight from the forward bending position of the back to reduce the pain.

Severe spasm occurs due to extreme pain unless complete bed rest is given. The pain is severe and increases if complete bed rest is not taken. The whole backbone becomes stiff and tender from a sharp localized pain in that area. This leads the patient to become irritable and depressed.

Treatment

To reduce the pain the patient would need administration of analgesics by oral tablets or injections. Complete bed rest for 8 -10 days is advised for effective management of pain during acute stage. Select suitable asanas from the following list and practice under proper guidance.

Asanas

1. Ardha-Halasana
2. Setubandhasana
3. Makarasana,
4. Niralambasana,
5. Ardha Shalabhasana
6. Brahmamudra,
7. Parvatasana,
8. Tadasana.
9. Supta-tadasana,
10. Chakrasana (Sideward bending)
11. Shavasana,

Pranayama : Anuloma-Viloma Pranayama

Om Recitation.

Observe these points carefully

1. One should avoid jerky and hasty movements of the spine
2. Patients are advised to avoid forward bending at least initially for first 2-3 months after the episode of the prolapse of the disc.
3. The postures should be modified as per the need and capacity of the person.
4. Patient should avoid long hours of sitting or standing
5. Use of lumbar belt is advised during traveling and movements.

6. Morning walk will be beneficial.
7. Avoid overeating and massage.
8. Use hard bed for sleeping.
9. Do not sleep with straight legs in supine condition. Fold one leg or both legs or sleep on any one side.

Avoid lifting the weight from the ground straight way unless the individual bends over the knees and brings the weight nearer to the body.

6. Varicose Veins

Varicose Veins are the dilated and tortuous, enlarged veins, particularly at the back of the legs. They are common in middle aged and elderly people. People who have to stand for a prolong period at one place or required to carry heavy weight for a long distance on their shoulders or head are prone to develop varicose veins.

Causes

The defective valves in the long veins of the legs like long sephanous vein cause the backward flow of blood from the thighs downward giving rise to sustained accumulation of the blood leading to elongation and tortuosity in the portion of the sephanous vein in the ankle, back region of the calf muscles, back of the knee joints and inner aspect of the thigh. The squeezing action of the calf muscles is also not sufficient. Therefore blood does not return back properly to the heart. During pregnancy also temporary varicosity of the long veins of the legs occur as a result of compression of the inferior vena cava by the pressure of the growing uterus. Valvular competence usually is re-established after pregnancy. Tumors obstructing blood flow can also cause varicose veins. When there is a thrombosis (blockage) in the deep veins of the legs, there is increased load on the superficial veins to return the blood to the heart leading to varicosity.

Signs and Symptoms

Patients usually complain fatigue and discomfort in the

legs by standing for a long period. There is a sharp localized pain in the sites of the varicose veins, swelling of the ankles, itching of the skin over the legs is produced by the end of the day. Ulceration of the skin over legs and feet occur in cases of varicosity of long standing.

Treatment

Patients with marked reduction of their activity from the discomfort of the varicose veins need to undergo operative intervention. However cases that are not very severe can be treated by conservative means like keeping the legs raised from the ground and keeping over the stool. Application of crape bandage or use of elastic stockings up to the region of thigh during walking is helpful in minimizing the symptoms of varicose veins. For mild and moderate varicose veins, suitable asanas and other yoga practices may be selected. Inverted poses like viparita karani are immensely helpful.

Asanas : Sarvangasana, Shirshasana, Viparitakarani.

These are most helpful asanas provided they are performed under proper guidance of an expert yoga teacher and the patient should have no health problems like hypertension and cervical spondylitis.

Asanas from the following list may be practiced which would help in improving the venous return from the legs by contraction of the muscles, as per the capacity of the patient.

Tadasana, Paschimottanasana, Pavanamuktasana, Janushirasana, Gomukhasana, Vajrasana, Supta Vajrasana,

Shashankasana, Shavasana.

Suryanamaskaras are also beneficial.

Points to be noted

1. Avoid standing for long time. While walking put the heel first on the ground and then the toes.
2. Keep the legs elevated in the night with the support of the pillow to drain the accumulated blood from the veins.
3. During pregnancy sleep on the side to aid venous return by shifting the pressure on the inferior vena cava.
4. Use elastic pressure bandage or elastic stockings.
5. Do not practice asanas by just watching T.V. Or reading books.
6. Learn them from proper Yoga Therapist and practice them carefully and cautiously.
7. Walking and swimming are also helpful.
8. Extend and stretch the legs alternately in sitting position. Make circular movements of the legs. For people having sedentary job long sitting should take a stool in front of their chair to remove the pressure on the back of the thigh. During work they should move frequently within the working place to stimulate the venous return.
9. Take simple vegetarian diet without much spices.

7. Backache

Backache is a vague term, which indicates pain any where in the back region, without mentioning the cause. There is a dull, continuous pain and tenderness in the back muscles, especially in the lumbar, lumbo-sacral or in the upper region of the spine.

Causes of backache

Causes of backache are varied such as Spondylosis, spondylitis, spondylolisthesis, slipped disc, strain, sprain, spasm, and weak abdominal or back muscles. However the main reason related to the conditions mentioned above is a faulty posture of the individual during various activities like sitting, standing, walking, sleeping and lifting the weight from the ground. Backache may also be due to structural changes at various levels of spine due to accident resulting in spinal injury including fracture. Backache may be a 'referred pain' due to diseases of internal organs like pelvic infection of the uterus or the fallopian tubes and the ovary. It may also be from the secondary deposits of lesions of the cancer of the stomach, liver, ovaries and uterus. Psychological problems like anxiety, depression, mental tension, emotional stress, also lead to backache and emotional stress and tendency to avoid work in which the individual is not interested. Physical stress from heavy muscular work may result in backache. Obesity and overweight adds to the extra load to be borne by the spine, giving rise to backache.

Signs and Symptoms

There is a dull, continuous or acute unbearable pain or chronic bearable and long lasting pain in the affected region of the back. Patients also complain of heaviness, numbness, tingling sensation in hands and legs by pressure on the respective nerves. Pain along the sciatic nerve is also present in cases suffering from low back region. Patient is unable to sit, stand walk, and sleep comfortably. Spasm of the muscles of the back is often noticed during examination of these patients.

Treatment

Conventional treatment includes reduction in pain and discomfort with the help of analgesics, muscle relaxants, fomentation, orthopedic supports like belts etc. Psychotherapy is given when excessive muscle spasm is due to strong emotional disturbance known from the history of the illness.

Asanas

Suitable asanas from the list given below are found useful in managing these cases.

Tadasana, Chakrasana (Sideward bending in standing), Parvatasana, Vakrasana Brahmamudra, Ardha-Shalabhasana, Niralambasana, Pavanamuktasana, Ardha-halasana, Setubandh-asana, Makarasana, Gomukhasana, crocodile postures in different variations and Shavasana are recommended.

Pranayama

Anuloma-Viloma Pranayama (minimum 10 rounds)

Om chanting should be recited minimum ten times.

Follow these points carefully

1. Use hard bed for sleeping.
2. Do not sleep on the back with legs fully stretched. Keep them slightly bent and together or sleep on any one side by folding one or both the legs.
3. Lift equal weight in both hands by bending in the lumbar as well as in knees while lifting.

Do not stop or reduce the medicines on your own without consulting your doctor from whom the treatment is taken.

8. HYPERTENSION

Hypertension is getting a prominent place in the list of causes of death. Hypertension should not be considered as a disease in the regular sense but as a state in which systolic blood pressure is maintained above 140 mmHg or more and diastolic blood pressure more than 90 mmHg. It is called **essential hypertension** when no specific cause is known and **secondary hypertension** when it is associated with kidney function impairment and increased peripheral spasm due to sympathetic overpowering on account of stress and rarely due to tumors like pheochromocytoma or endocrinal disorders involving the adrenals.

Maintenance of normal blood pressure (BP) depends upon balance between cardiac output and peripheral vascular resistance. Peripheral resistance is determined by the intensity of smooth muscle contraction of arterioles. Normally a delicate balance is maintained between sympathetic and parasympathetic nervous control. Persistent raised BP can cause cerebral ischaemia, paralytic attack, and acute myocardial infarction leading to sudden death. Ocular blood vessel damage from atherosclerotic changes will result in retinal detachment and problems of vision.

Causes

Apart from stress, lack of physical exercise, overweight, faulty dietary habits, smoking lead to hardening of the arterial wall. This narrowing of peripheral blood vessels gives rise to increased peripheral vascular resistance thereby leading to an increase in systolic and diastolic blood pressure. Angina at different levels, renal function impairment, renal failure, peripheral vascular diseases from atherosclerotic changes will lead to secondary hypertension.

Signs and Symptoms

Systolic blood pressure increases above 140-mmHg and Diastolic blood pressure increases above 90 mmHg. Patient is restless because of feeling of heaviness in the head. Pathological changes in various organs resulting from deposits of cholesterol on the inner wall of the blood vessels leading to narrowing of the diameter may give rise to reduction of blood supply and functional disorders.

Yogic Treatment

Conventional treatment consists of BP reducing drugs under various groups such as diuretics, beta-blockers, calcium antagonists, and pace inhibitors. Each one of them is however known to have certain side effects, which makes the individual uncomfortable. Moreover these drugs bring only the BP under control but are not able to stop the pathological changes in various organs. Yoga on the other hand, by its holistic approach produces sustained fall in BP without any side effects. Yoga actually brings about changes in the individual at physical, mental, emotional, social and spiritual levels from various practices and should be seen as a way of life and not as a treatment. Generally following yoga practices are advised.

Asanas

Cultural asanas like Vrikshasana, Tadasana, Vajrasana,

Gomukhasana, Ardha-Matsyendrasana, Vakrasana, Makarasana, Ardha-Shalabhasana and Sarvangasana are advised which are known to have beneficial effect in reducing the blood pressure. Meditative posture like Padmasana, Siddhasana are also known to bring about control in blood pressure by inhibiting the thought process by leading the individual towards Dhyan. Most important is Shavasana to produce prolonged relaxative state of mind, as well as, relaxation of the blood vessels of all the extremities.

Pranayama

Yogic breathing techniques like Anuloma viloma, Ujjayi, Sitkari, Shitali, Bhramari. (10 rounds of selected pranayama) are found beneficial in controlling the blood pressure. Long practice of pranayama has been found to reduce the metabolic activity leading to more parasympathetic predominance.

Omkar recitation : (10 to 20 times)

Meditation : (for 10 to 20 min.)

Points to be observed

1. Do not stop the medicines abruptly unless advised by the doctor.
2. Avoid spicy and excessively oily foods. Whole grain food should be preferred. Avoid fast foods.
3. Regular timings for meals should be observed. Meals after 10 p.m. should be discouraged as the gap between the night meal and sleep should be at least more than 2 hours.

4. Yogic practices should be learnt from an authentic Yoga therapist.
5. The beneficial effect of yogic practices is seen only when they are performed regularly and for a prolonged period and practiced in a proper manner.
6. Avoid smoking and alcohol.
7. Change in outlook towards the life by living in a tension free atmosphere and having mental equipoise in times of conflicts and stresses is necessary.
8. Positive thinking and peaceful state of mind through out a day will bring the best control on the hypertension.

9. Diabetes

Diabetes mellitus is not a disease but a chronic disorder of carbohydrate metabolism where glucose is not taken up by the cells of the body from the blood. Glucose provides energy to the cells of all the organs of the body to perform their functions. The entry of glucose into the cell from the blood is helped by insulin, secreted from islets of Langerhans located in pancreas. The cells become ineffective to the presence of circulating insulin in number of people after middle age while certain people have deficiency of insulin secretion because of certain diseases of beta cells of islets of Langerhans. Both these conditions lead to increase of blood sugar in the circulation, which is known as diabetes mellitus.

As we all know the normal fasting blood sugar range is 80 to 120 mg per 100 ml of blood and post prandial blood sugar after two hours of meals should be up to 140 mg / 100 ml of blood. Persons who are not within this range are considered as diabetic.

Causes

Diabetes is classified in to 1) Insulin Dependent Diabetes Mellitus (IDDM) or type I and Non Insulin Dependent Diabetes Mellitus (NIDDM) or type II diabetes. When diabetes occurs in childhood it is known as *Juvenile diabetes.* Diabetes found in middle-aged people is known as *Maturity onset diabetes.* Other associated conditions are heredity, obesity, mental and emotional stress and strain, prolonged anxiety and conflict, sedentary lifestyle, lack of exercise and wrong food habits.

Signs and Symptoms

On many occasions persons are detected to be diabetic when they approach doctor for other complaints like fever not responding to the treatment or when they approach the doctor for medical check up to take life insurance policy. Main signs are, elevated blood sugar level (hyperglycemia) fasting as well as post prandial, appearance of sugar in urine (glycosuria), excessive urine production (polyurea) and hence frequent urination. Juvenile diabetic people are known to have excessive hunger and thirst, itching especially of the genitals and other parts of the covered skin, headache, vomiting, weakness and debility, sweating, palpitation, loss of weight, eye disorders, tremor, dizziness, staggering, acidosis due to excessive production of ketone bodies. Coma (prolonged unconscious state) is the last and the most severe state.

Treatment

Diabetes is considered as a state with which one has to bear up to the end of life. However, proper exercise, control of diet, hygienic measures like taking gargles and skin care will keep majority of symptoms under control. Oral anti diabetic tablets in persons whose blood sugar doesn't come under control with diet and exercise are advised.

Insulin injection is required in patients whose endogenous insulin secretion is deficient due to destruction of beta cells of islets of Langerhans. In yogic treatment consisting of relaxative asanas and the advice to change the outlook in our day-to-day life bring about control of sugar. However since the stress aspect of this psychosomatic condition and the efficacy of yoga in controlling have been recognized, the management of the disorder has become easy.

Yogic treatment

Along with the well-balanced diet, medicine and a few exercises, necessary corrections in lifestyle and the following yoga practices will help the patients to manage the disorder successfully. Patient should be educated about the overall situation and convinced that the treatment will have to be continued for rest of the life.

Asanas

Bhujangasana, Shalabhasana, Dhanurasana, Naukasana, Pavanmuktasana, Ushtrasana, Vrikshasana, Vakrasana, Shavasana, Sarvangasana or Viparita karani, Matsyasana, Halasana, Ardha-matsyendrasana.

Kriyas

Neti, Vaman or Vastra dhauti, Kapalabhati, Nauli and Agnisara.

Pranayama

Anuloma-Viloma, Ujjayi, Bhramari (minimum 10 rounds of each)

Om recitation : (10 rounds or more)

Meditation : (10 to 20 minutes)

Helpful tips

1. Try to remain mentally relaxed through out the day.
2. Avoid high calorie carbohydrates / oily foods. Consume protein rich diet.

3. Think positively and observe Healthy Life Style.
4. Perform moderate exercises to adjust calorie consumption.
5. Practice yoga regularly with patience.

Frequent monitoring of blood glucose level and adjustment of the medicinal dosages should be done as per the doctor's advice.

10. Indigestion, Constipation and Flatulence

Efficient digestive system is necessary for sound health. If the process of digestion is not complete the undigested food is fermented. Several symptoms like pain, belching, nausea, heartburn due to acid regurgitation into esophagus and accumulation of gas are experienced. This is called as **indigestion (Dyspepsia).**

Flatulence is the condition where there is a distension of the stomach or colon due to accumulated gas. Excess production of gas or less absorption of gas in the gastro-intestinal tract may be relieved through the mouth or the anus.

Difficult defecation that requires force to clear the bowels may be due to sluggish action of the bowels. This is known as **Constipation.** Generally, two to three times bowel movements in a day are considered as 'normal' for the healthy individual.

Causes

Eating too much, too often or irregularly, improper chewing due to hurried eating, lack of exercise, air swallowed unknowingly while eating and drinking, consumption of junk food are the causes of indigestion. Liver function disorder is commonly associated with complaints of the indigestion. This also leads to flatulence in some people and constipation in others. Weak abdominal tone and lowered intestinal motility, worry, anxiety, fear, insomnia, are some of the other causes of indigestion, constipation and flatulence. The bowel movements are not regular in constipated persons, particularly in persons who are having sedentary job, lack of exercise and inadequate intake of water.

Signs and Symptoms

There is fullness of abdomen observed in people suffering from indigestion and flatulence. Gas passes from mouth or anus. There is a pain in stomach or uneasiness if the gas is not passed and bowels are not properly evacuated. Persons suffering from constipation, pass stools that are dry and hard and have to strain while passing stools. Dry and hard stools lead to injury to the anal canal which known as fissure. Anxiety, worries, belching, bad breathe, dyspepsia, headache, acidity are some of the associated symptoms. Persons suffering from chronic constipation may develop hernia whose abdominal musculature is weak.

Treatment

A proper diet, exercise, adequate intake of water usually would prevent the occurrence of these above complaints. Some of them would feel better by administration of oral vitamins and enzymes and mild laxatives. The following yogic practices are recommended along with the general measures.

Kriyas

1. Laghoo Shankhaprakshalan, Kunjala
2. Vamana or Ganesha Kriya whenever necessary.
3. Kapalabhati
4. Agnisara (mild)

5. Nauli after drinking warm water.

Asanas

Trikonasana, Pada-hastasana, Vajrasana, (after meals for 10 minutes), Naukasana in prone position, Niralambasana, Vipritakarani, Makarasana, Shashankasana, Parvatasana, Pavanamuktasana, Shavasana.

Pranayama

Anulom-Vilom (10 rounds) Ujjayi pranayama (10 rounds)

Om Recitation : 10 -20 times

Meditation : 10 -20 minutes

11. Menstrual Disorders

A periodic discharge of a bloody fluid from the uterus occurring at more or less at regular interval of 28 days in women from the age of puberty to menopause is known as menstruation. The flow of altered blood along with endometrial and stoma cells, glandular secretion and occasional blood clots occurs for 3 to 5 days through a vaginal passage. Menstruation ceases during pregnancy. Its failure to occur may result from some abnormalities, physical disorders, emotional and hormonal disturbances.

Common menstrual disorders are as follows:

1. Amenorrhea

It is the absence of menstruation. It may be caused by a hormonal imbalance, obesity or extreme weight loss, emotional disorders (excitement, anorexia nervosa) etc.

2. Menorrhagia

There is an excessive bleeding during monthly menstrual periods, in terms of more days as well as the amount of blood. Disturbances in pituitary, thyroid and ovary functions, hypertension, and diabetes mellitus are the main causes.

3. Metrorrhagia

There is excessive flow of blood occurring between two menstrual periods. The main causes are poor functioning of ovaries, pituitary and thyroid glands, poor blood clotting function, some psychological factors, and lesions of the cervix. Malignancy of the genital tract should be excluded.

4. Dysmenorrhea

Pain & discomfort is felt prior to the onset of or at the time of menstruation. Discomfort is mainly in the lower abdomen, pain in thighs and a general feeling of pressure. Causes of Dysmenorrhea are anatomical malformation like undeveloped womb, pathological changes in pelvis, hormonal disturbances and mental factors. Sometimes, when pain is severe, other complaints such as nausea, vomiting or headache interfere with the normal activities.

5. Pre-Menstrual Tension

Many women suffer from this complaint for a week or 10 days before the onset of menstruation. The symptoms are headache, tremors, irritability, heaviness in breasts and pelvic region.

6. Leucorrhoea

White or yellowish mucous discharge during the first half of the cycle from the vagina is most normal. Secretions become more this at the time of ovulation. However, an excessive white discharge becomes the problem when it is associated with irritation or itching due to fungus infection of the vaginal canal. Leucorrhoeal discharge is associated with offensive odor. There is an infection due to trichomonas *vaginalis.*

Signs and Symptoms

The condition of Amenorrhea may not be having any particular symptom except obesity resulting from hormonal disorder. Women suffering from Menorrhagia and Metrorrhagia complain of pain and weakness and may be unable to carry routine work in case the bleeding is severe. Dysmenorrhea is associated with presence of pain in the lower back and hypogastrium.

Causes of Menstrual disorder

Faulty development of reproductive organs, imbalance of hormones of endocrine glands (specially reproductive), weak muscles of reproductive organs, weak constitution, pathological development and psychological disturbances like depression, fear, stress and mental tension are the main causes.

Yogic Management

Regular and proper practice of asanas and Pranayama is beneficial to all women especially for those suffering from menstrual disorders. However, it should be noted that, during monthly period (menstruation) yoga practices are not advisable for 3-5 days. Proper rest, best hygiene, medicines, relaxation are also necessary. Yoga helps by correcting and balancing the functioning of the endocrine system, toning up of the nervous system, by relaxing the body and mind thereby reducing the psychological problems.

Asanas

Following asanas are usually recommended during the interval between two menstrual cycles.

Tadasana, Vrikshasana, Chakrasana (sideward bonding), Trikonasana, Bhujangasana, Ardhashalabhasana, Ardhahalasana with one and two legs, Viparitakarani, Sarvangasana followed by matsyasana, Naukasana on the back (Dronasana), Pavanamuktasana, Setubandhasana, Vajrasana, Padmasana, Parvatasana, Vakrasana, Gomukhasana, Shavasana, Makarasana.

Pranayama : Anuloma Viloma, Shitali, Bhramari

Om recitation and Meditation.

Points to be noted

1. Correct approach to life, regular diet, exercise and hygiene are very essential for normal development and functioning of the reproductive organs.
2. Asanas are helpful to preserve the general health and to reduce the minor complaints regarding menstruation by improving the vigor and strength of the body.

General principles to be followed

Special Hints

1. The number and the sequence of yoga practices should to be modified according to the capacity and other conditions of the person.
2. Avoid practicing yoga by only observing T.V. or by reading a book on therapy.
3. The practices should be learnt from a qualified Yoga therapist.
4. Take rest either in *Shavasana* or Makarasana in between two asanas. At the end, practice Shavasana at least for 15-20 minutes.
5. Observe effortlessness, comfort, stability, while performing yoga practices.
6. Concentrate on stretching and breathing movements during the practice to avoid distraction.
7. Take moderate vegetarian diet. Fill half stomach with food, one forth with water and leave one forth space for proper churning of the food.
8. Include yoga in your daily routine and accept it as a life style. Patience and regular practice is necessary.
9. Always try to keep balance on right and left sides while standing.

12. Anxiety and Obesity

Anxiety is a central cause of Neurosis and is commonly seen as a result of excessive psychosomatic stress. Anxiety is the normal reaction to the anticipated thinking related to the future about self, loved ones and the life, career, earnings etc. Certain amount of anxiety is normal that motivates the individual for planning and execution of the systematic work. Excessive anxiety however, interferes with the normal efficiency of a person. Chronic anxiety is a major contributory factor to many other psychosomatic disorders like hypertension, ischaemic heart disease, obesity, asthma, and diabetes.

Cause

Heredity, constant emotional disturbance, fear or fright in especially neglected or overprotected children and youngsters, unsuccessful love affair, disappointment on failure in one's career. Anticipatory fear or worry about work, function, journey etc.

Many times the patient is aware of the causes but is helpless in the management. If not properly treated in an early stage the condition may lead to the development of neurosis. Nervous apprehension before any work causes anxiety.

Signs and Symptoms

Patient feels constantly anxious. He or she is highly tense or panicky about the events in future. There is a feeling of tightness in the chest, which may be associated with the difficulty in swallowing or breathing. Tachycardia with mental agitation, Pain in the chest, tension headache, pain in the joints and trembling in the limbs, tremors in hands and fingers, excessive perspiration, flushing of the face are some of the symptoms. Accelerated thoracic breathing, difficulty in rational thinking, lack of concentration and frequent urination are other important symptoms. Systolic blood pressure is raised up to 140-150 mmHg.

Yogic Treatment

Shifting of awareness consciously from thoracic breathing to the abdominal breathing helps a lot in reducing anxiety. Counseling by near one also helps. Diversion of thought process, humor or participation in children's play relieves the tensions and anxiety.

Kriyas : Jala neti, Trataka, Agnisara (Mild)

Asanas

Vipritakarani, Ardha-halasana, Pavanmuktasana, Bhujangasana, Makarasana, Ardha-shalabhasana, Vakrasana, Parvatasana, Gomukhasana, Chakrasana, Tadasana, Trikonasana, Vrikshasana, Shavasana. Practice of Surya-namaskar is also helpful.

Mudras : Brahmamudra.

Bandhas : Uddiyana

Pranayama : Anuloma-Viloma, Bhramari, and Ujjayi.

Om recitation (10 times or more) and meditation

Points to be noted:

(1) Do not neglect your feelings and experiences. Consult the elderly persons at home.

(2) During asanas the attention should be focused on the breathing process.

(3) Regularity, patience, perseverance and belief in yoga practices is necessary.

(4) Control or express your emotions, do not suppress them. Think positively.

(5) Have light and easily digestible diet. Avoid milk and milk products, rice, curd, banana, sour fruits and fried items.

(6) In case of panic situation concentrate on the abdominal breathing, particularly on the complete exhalation.

(7) When the mind is restless, worried, if possible walk in the green woods.

(8) Remain engaged in some constructive work.

(9) Avoid cold drinks. Drink warm water instead of frequent tea or coffee.

(10) Shavasana and Om recitation is found very useful in such cases.

OBESITY

Obesity means fatness. The person looks very fat. There is an excessive accumulation of fat in the body. The fat is mainly deposited in the subcutaneous tissue (under the skin) particularly at the waist, thighs and abdomen, omentum, mesentery as well as around the heart and liver. It is a common metabolic disorder found in all ages and in both sexes. It becomes a social stigma due to disproportionate and unattractive appearance. Due to large surface area of the body or the body mass, an extra load is imposed on respiratory, circulatory and excretory systems. Therefore any imbalance in the functions of these systems would reduce the vitality and weaken the immune system. That is why obesity generally leads to disorders like hypertension, anxiety, asthma and diabetes. Obesity also reduces cardiovascular endurance or stamina and several other capacities. The fatty person cannot walk or run fast due to overweight and immediately becomes breathless.

Causes

The main cause of obesity is overeating, eating without hunger and consumption of wrong type of food that is mostly spicy, oily with surplus carbohydrates. This disturbs the balance between the caloric intake and utilization of the calories. The intake is in excess of the body's need and there is lack of exercise due to sedentary and luxurious lifestyle. The result is 'gain in the weight' and size. Overeating can also be due to depression, mental and emotional disturbances. Disorder of the ductless glands such as thyroid, pituitary and gonads may also be the factor.

Heredity is another contributing factor.

Signs and Symptoms

Weight is excessively high. Person becomes lethargic and dull. There is no inertia or willingness for strenuous work. Body looks puffy and flabby. Fat accumulates around the abdomen, neck, hips and thighs. Shape of the body is disproportionate. Anxiety and depression may be present. Other psychosomatic diseases may be associated viz. hypertension, diabetes or the glandular disorder like hypothyroidism.

Yogic treatment

Change in lifestyle is a 'must'. An obese person needs inspiration and willpower. Diet regulation is another most important remedy. Change of work, engaging oneself in creative or slight strenuous work like gardening, repairing or cleaning the house would consume some calories. Morning or evening walk, Surya namaskar and daily yoga practice, suggested below, is useful but a long way to change the wrong habits and to reestablish the metabolic and hormonal balance.

Shuddhi Kriyas : Vaman or Danda dhauti, Neti, Laghoo/ purna Shankhaprakshalana (once a week/month), Nauli, Agnisara, Kapalabhati if the blood pressure is normal.

Asanas

Ardha-halasana, Vipritakarani, Pavanmuktasana, Bhujangasana, Makarasana, Ardha-shalabhasana, Dhanurasana, Vakrasana, Parvatasana, Gomukhasana, Paschimottana, Ushtrasana, Chakrasana (sideward bending), Tadasana, Trikonasana, Vrikshasana, Shavasana. Practice of Surya-namaskar is also helpful.

Mudras : Yogamudra.

Bandhas : Uddiyana.

Pranayama : Anuloma-Viloma, Suryabhedana (more than 20 times) and Ujjayi pranayama (minimum 10 rounds).

Om recitation (10 times or more) and meditation

Diet: Mitahara- ½ stomach should be filled with food, ¼ with water and ¼ part should remain empty. Avoid excessive intake of sugar (sweets), oily and spicy food and non-vegetarian food. Do not consume milk products and food prepared with refined floor (bakery bread). Take more salads, sprouted cereals and green vegetables.

Points to be noted

1. The medical check up and advice from a doctor is necessary before starting yoga. Presence of other psychosomatic disorder like hypertension, diabetes will change the yogic regime.
2. Meals should be taken at regular timings. Food having more roughage and less oil is advisable.
3. Avoid sitting idle. Engage yourself in some work that will exert you a little.
4. Regularity, patience and perseverance in yoga practices is necessary.

5. Avoid milk and milk products, rice, curd, banana, sour fruits and fried items.

Avoid bakery products and cold drinks. Drink warm water instead of frequent tea or coffee.

Special Hints

1. The number and the sequence of yoga practices should to be modified according to the capacity and other conditions of the person.
2. Avoid practicing yoga by only observing T.V. or by reading a book on therapy.
3. The practices should be learnt from a qualified Yoga therapist.
4. Take rest either in *Shavasana* or Makarasana in between two asanas. At the end, practice Shavasana at least for 15-20 minutes.
5. Observe effortlessness, comfort and stability, while performing yoga practices.
6. Concentrate on stretching and breathing movements during the practice to avoid distraction.
7. Take moderate vegetarian diet. Fill half stomach with food, one forth with water and leave one forth space for proper churning of the food.
8. Include yoga in your daily routine and accept it as a life style. Patience and regular practice is necessary.
9. Always try to keep balance on right and left sides while standing.

10. Brisk morning walk, games like long tennis, swiming are also healpful.

Please Note :

Yogic Treatment is available along with the dietary regime and naturopathy at **Health care center, Kaivalyadhama, Lonavla (Maharashtra).** Please inquire regarding booking and charges on **Phone: 02114-273039** or visit our Website:**www.kdham.com**

1. Shirshasana

2. Ardhahalasana

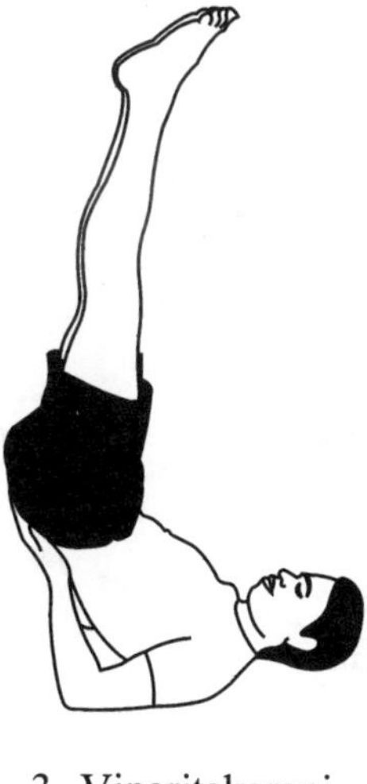

3. Viparitakarani

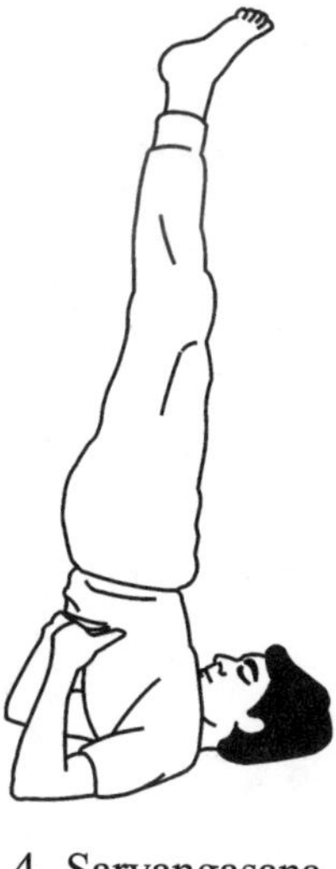

4. Sarvangasana

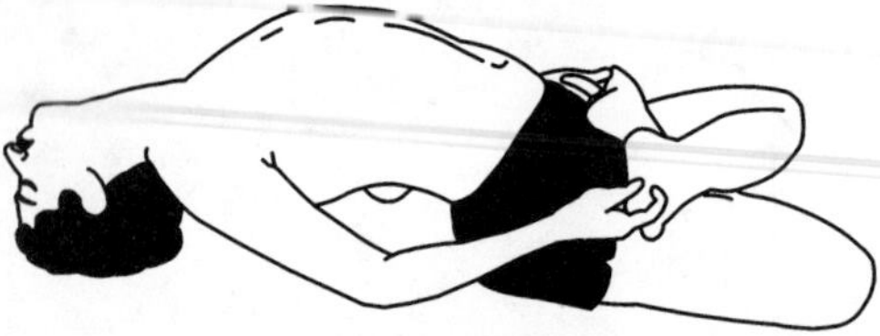

5. Matsyasana

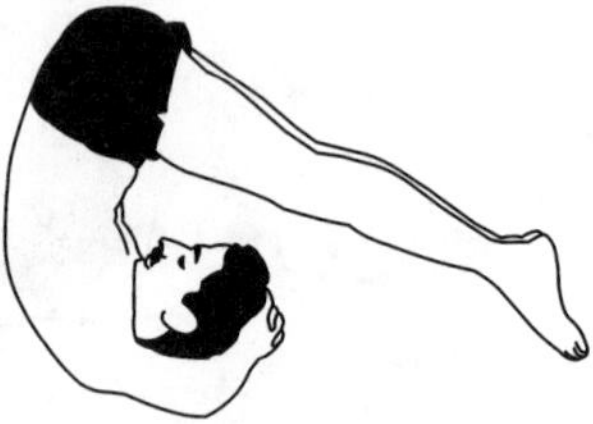

6. Halasana

7. Naukasana

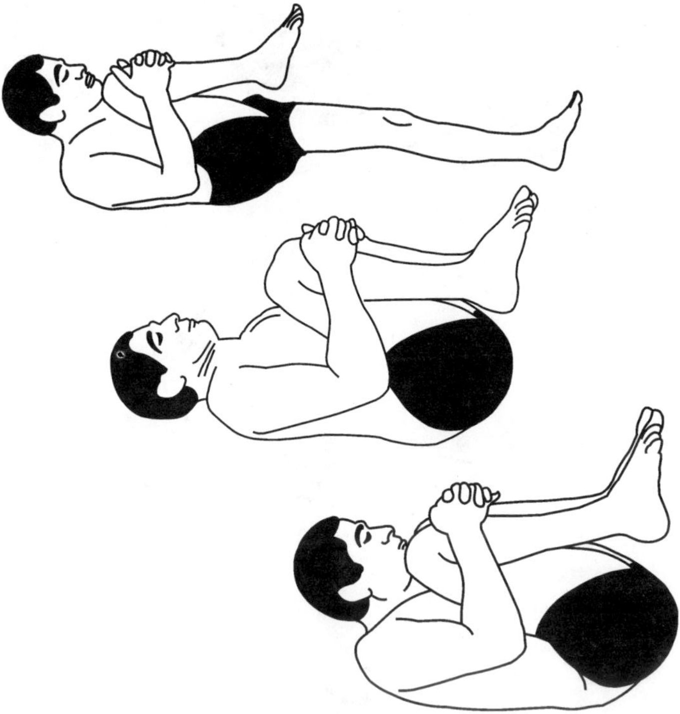

8. Pavana muktasana

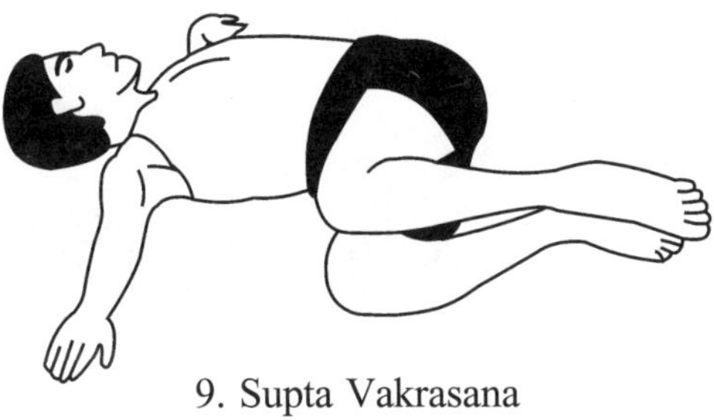

9. Supta Vakrasana

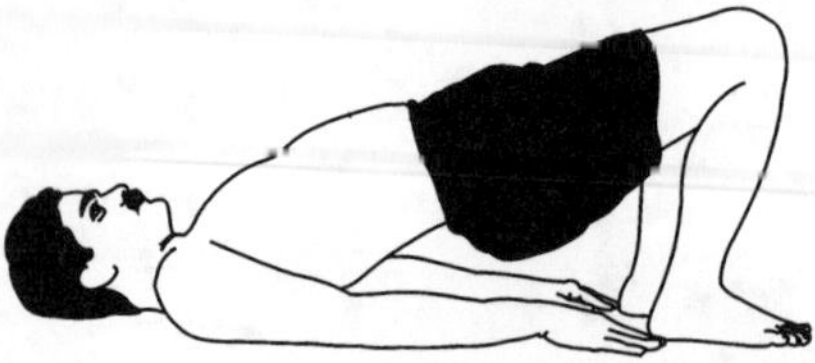

10. Setubandhasana

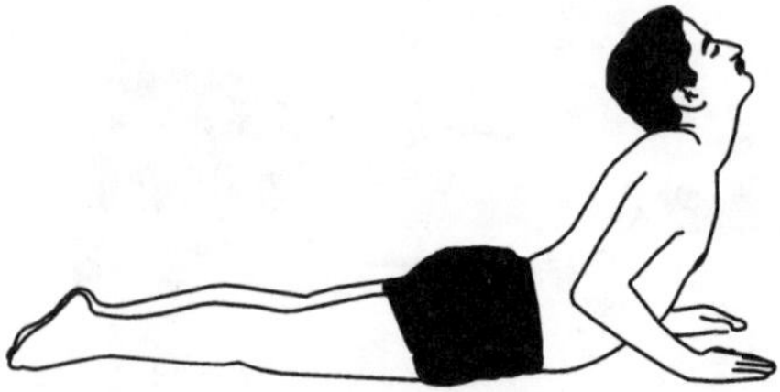

11. Bhujangasana

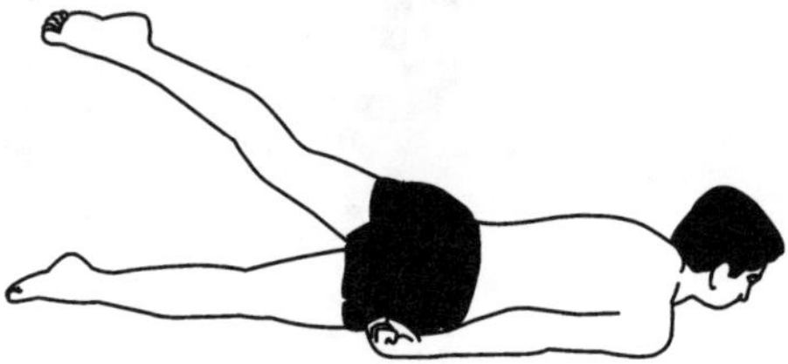

12. Ardha Shalbhasana

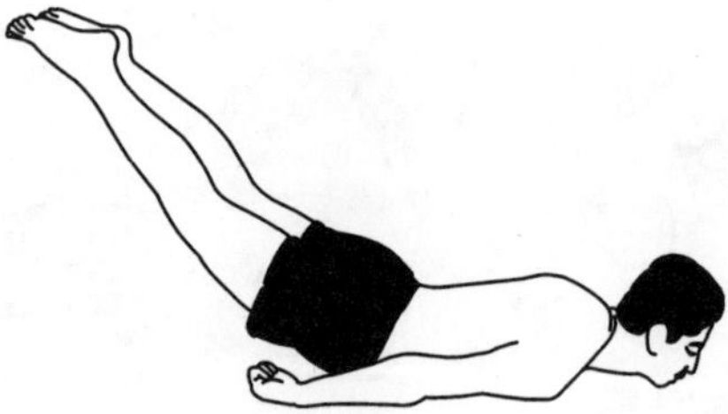

13. Shalbhasana

14. Dhanurasana

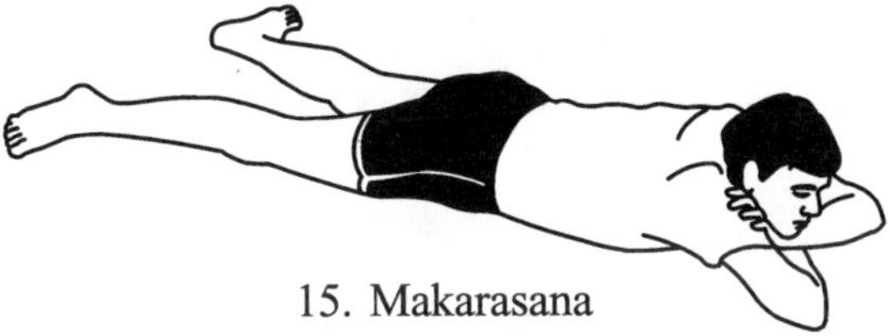

15. Makarasana

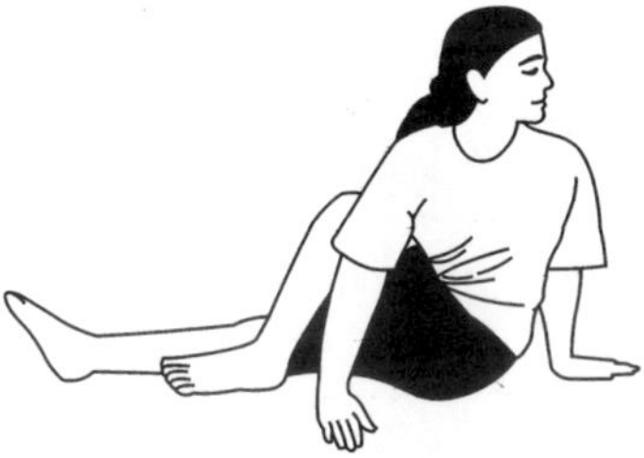

16. Vakrasana

17. Ardha Matsyendrasana

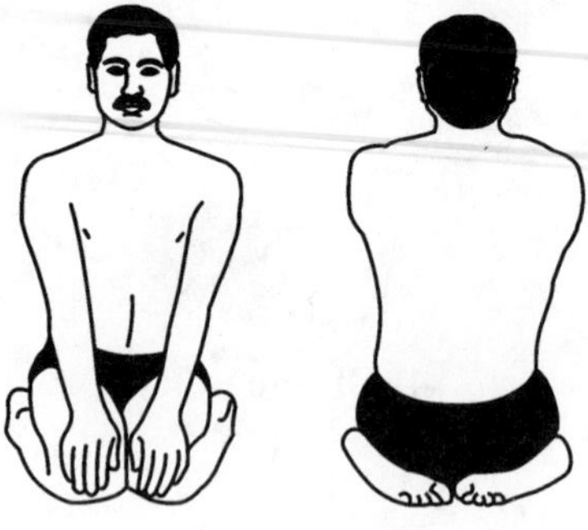

18. Vajrasana

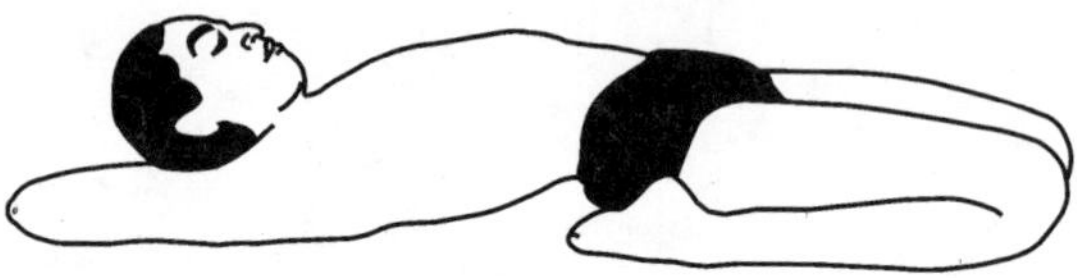

19. Supta Vjrasana

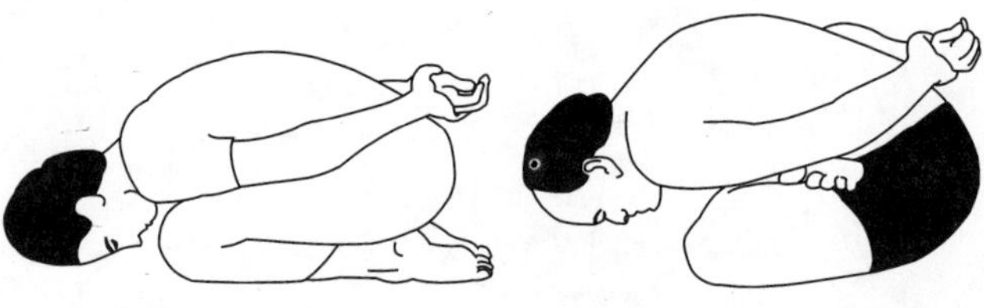

20. Yogamudra

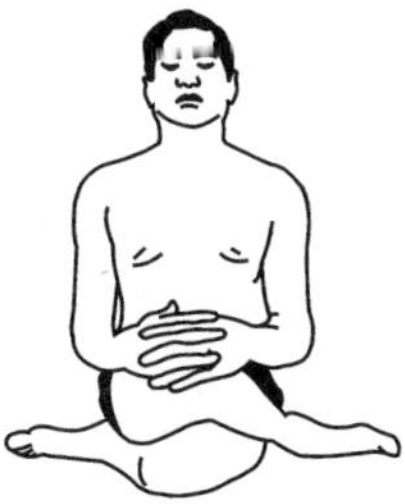

21. Gomukhasana

Front View

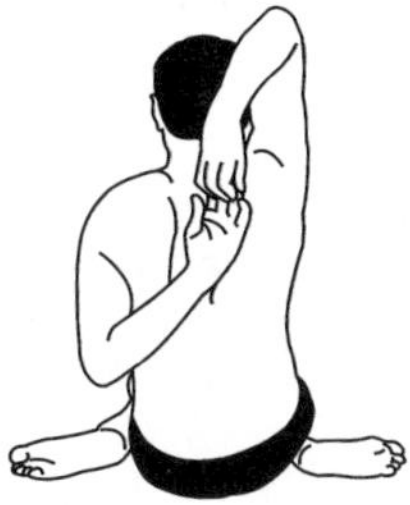

Back View

22. Parvatasana

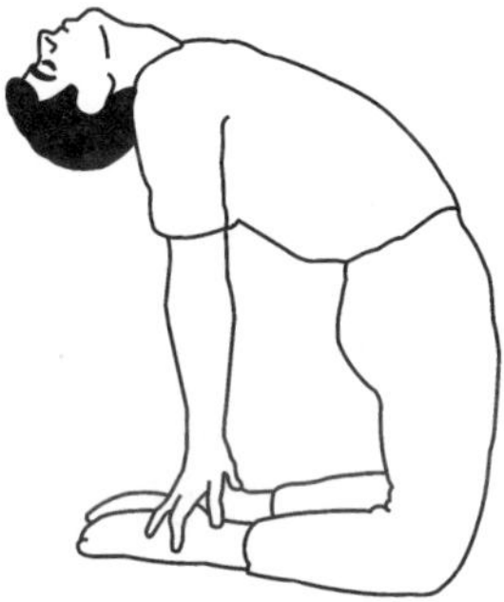

23. Ustrasana

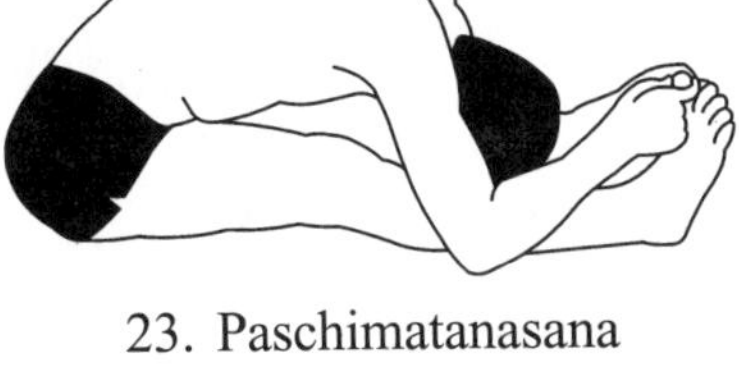

23. Paschimatanasana

24. Simhamudra

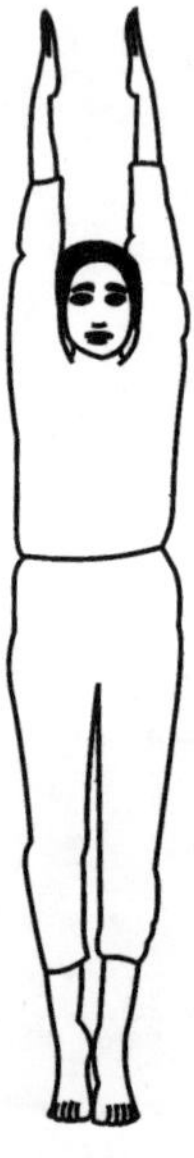

25. Tadasana

26. Chakrasana

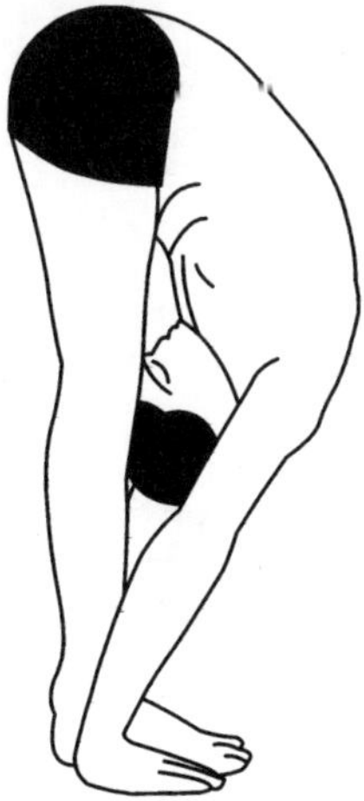

27. Pada Hastasana

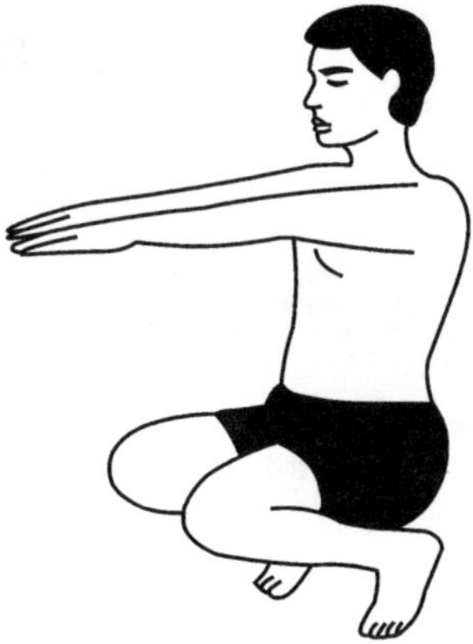

28. Utkatasana

29. Vrikshasana

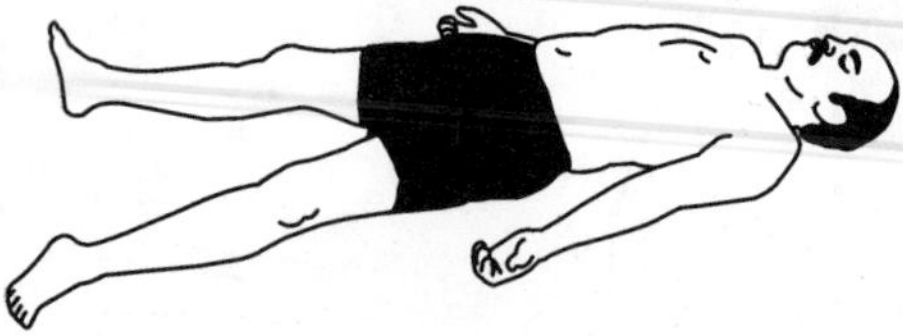

30. Shavasana

31. Ardha Padamasana

32. Padmasana

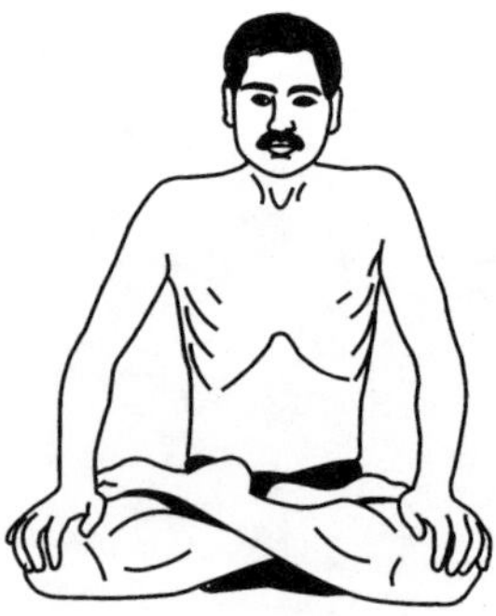

33. Kapalabhati

34. Jala Neti

35. Rubber Neti

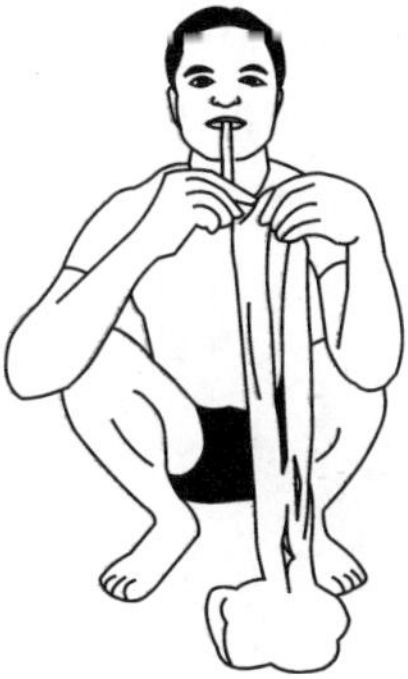

36. Vastra Dhauti

37. Jalandhar Bandha

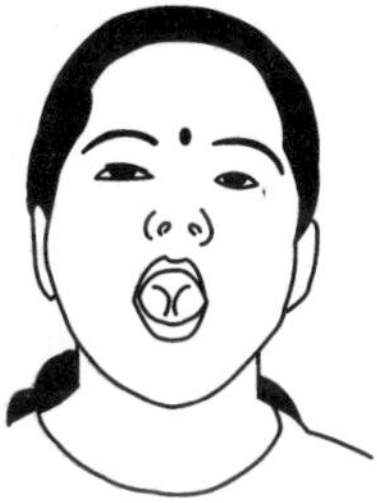

38. Jivabandha

39. Uddiyana Bandha

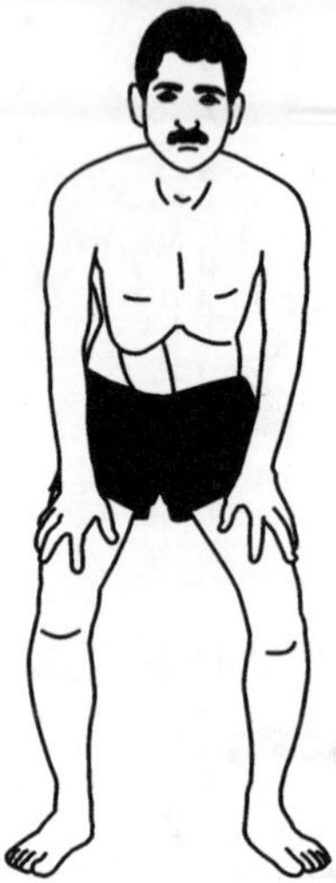

40. Right Nauli

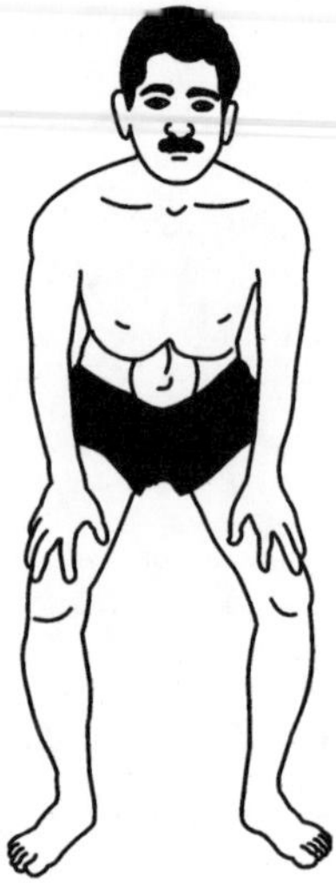

40. Central Nauli

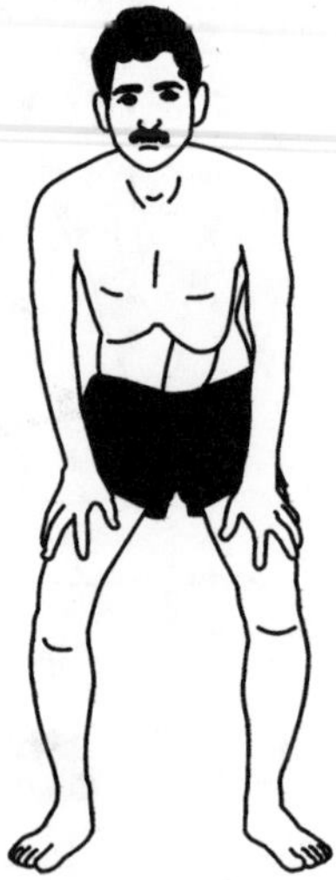

40. Left Nauli

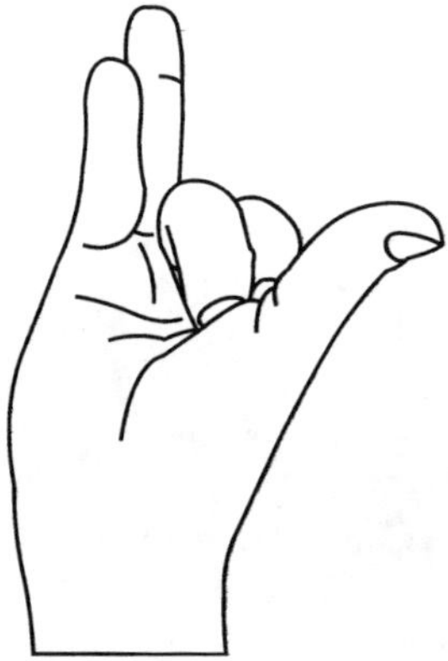

41. Pranav Mudra

42. Anulom Vilom